RUG
TUFTING
WITH SIMJI

Quarto.com
WalterFoster.com

© 2025 Quarto Publishing Group USA Inc.
Artwork & Text © 2025 SIMJI LLC

First Published in 2025 by Walter Foster Publishing, an imprint of The Quarto Group,
100 Cummings Center, Suite 265-D, Beverly, MA 01915, USA.
T (978) 282-9590 F (978) 283-2742

Walter Foster Publishing titles are also available at discount for retail, wholesale, promotional, and bulk purchase. For details, contact the Special Sales Manager by email at specialsales@quarto.com or by mail at The Quarto Group, Attn: Special Sales Manager, 100 Cummings Center, Suite 265-D, Beverly, MA 01915, USA.

29 28 27 26 25   1 2 3 4 5

ISBN: 978-0-7603-9109-9

Digital edition published in 2025
eISBN: 978-0-7603-9110-5

Library of Congress Cataloging-in-Publication Data is available.

Design: Amy Sly, The Sly Studio
Cover Image: SIMJI
Page Layout: The Sly Studio
Photography and project templates: SIMJI
Illustration: Veronica Carratello, except pages 11 and 28 by SIMJI

Printed in USA

RUG TUFTING
WITH SIMJI

Essential Techniques and
Creative Projects for Beginners

SIMJI

HELLO & WELCOME!

I'M SIMJI, AND I MAKE RUG CONTENT ON SOCIAL MEDIA. I'VE ENTERTAINED BILLIONS OF VIEWERS AND INTRODUCED THEM TO THE ART OF RUG TUFTING.

So how did I get into rug tufting, and then become a "rugfluencer" on social media? Believe it or not, it all began when I saw a random photo of a custom rug on Instagram. Before then, I'd never thought about how rugs were made, and the fact that they could be any shape other than a circle or square!

The fact that you could make your own RUGS seemed AMAZING to me and I wanted to try it so bad! So ... I went all in and bought the equipment in bulk. I had a plan to make rug content on social media and was determined to make my channel a success! Most people think the opposite, but I learned how to make rugs in order to make my content!

Before I knew it, I was the biggest and most followed rug content creator in the world, being invited to red carpet events in Hollywood and big companies like Coca-Cola, Netflix, Marvel, and many others wanting to work with me.

Now, thousands of rugs later, I still have to pinch myself when I think about how far I've come.

BUT WAIT, HAHA, what even is rug tufting?? Simply put, it is creating a rug with a handheld tufting gun. If you're new to rug tufting, and you want help getting started, you're in the right place. And if you've tufted a few times but can't seem to get your rugs to look "professional," I've got you covered, too!

Once you know the techniques, you'll be able to make all types of rugs no matter the shape or size. And in this book, you will discover just how creative you can be with rugs ... stepping into the untraditional and out of the box! Share your projects with me @simjiofficial on Instagram. I'd love to see what you make and I may share your creations!

Of course, I've made a lot of mistakes throughout my journey, from using the wrong materials to following poor technique. And my tufting guns have torn through a lot of fabric.

Little by little, though, I learned how to handle my tufting gun, and the more I practiced, the better my techniques became. Back when I first started, there was SO much misinformation about tufting. I really wish that I'd had someone who could teach me the foundation early on in my journey so I could have made fewer costly mistakes and saved some money, time, and physical pain lol. This is why I created this book for you.

First, we will go over some foundational techniques to put you ahead of the game! Then we'll work on ten projects that will help you explore your creativity as well as break your idea of what rugs can be! Together we'll build your confidence so that, once you've gone through this book, you can go on your own creative journey to tuft any project your heart desires.

I'll be right there with you the entire time and I've also included QR codes to videos of techniques and tips that you can refer to again and again ... and again!

So, without further ado, LET'S BEGIN!!!!

I made a lot of rugs and a LOT of mistakes!

BUT SOMEHOW IT ALL WORKED OUT!

TOOLS & MATERIALS

I've compiled a list of the tools you'll need to get started, such as a rug-tufting gun, a tufting frame, tufting cloth, yarn, glue, backing fabric, and other materials. I'll also explain the purpose of each item and what to look for when buying materials.

It's true that getting set up for rug tufting can be a little expensive—but it's so worth it. Keep in mind that you don't need the fanciest or most expensive rug-tufting tools to make great rug projects. So, when in doubt, go basic.

You can find all of the tools and materials that you'll need for the projects in this book either online or in a fabric store or craft store.

1. TUFTING GUN

Let's start with the fun stuff. The modern rug-tufting gun is a handheld power tool used to push yarn through a primary cloth (tufting cloth) to create a loop or cut-pile rug.

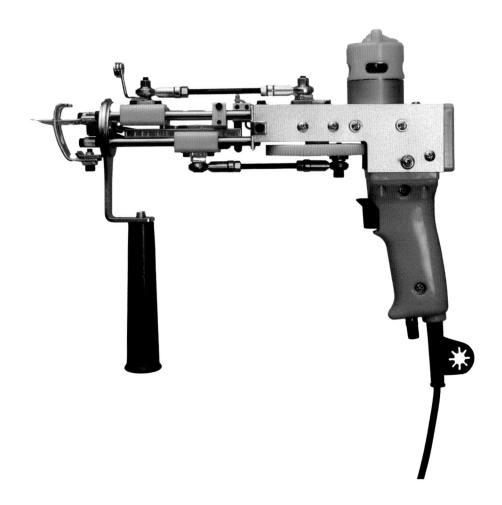

2. TUFTING FRAME

You'll need a tufting frame—usually a square wooden or metal frame that the tufting cloth is stretched on. You can buy freestanding frames, ones that get clamped to a table, or you can even make your own. I eventually made my own frame to accommodate the size of my larger pieces, but for the purpose of this book, I suggest getting a basic wood frame that's about 3 ft. x 3 ft. (.9 x .9 m). It's great for beginners who are just starting to get into tufting.

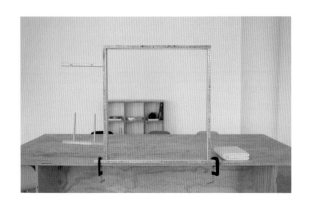

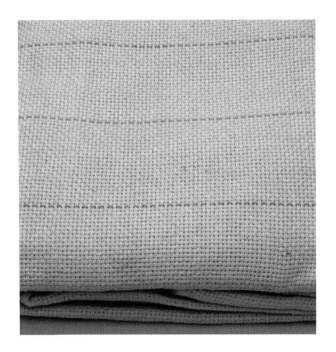

3. TUFTING CLOTH

We'll be using tufting cloth, also known as *primary tufting cloth* or *tufting fabric*, as the foundation for the tufted rugs in this book. This is stretched onto your tufting frame and will be your rug-making canvas. There are some that are a cotton and polyester blend and some that are 100 percent polyester. They may or may not have guide lines.

Fun Fact!

Did you know the first electric tufting gun was developed in Dalton, Georgia, United States in 1930?!

Tufting guns are being developed in many different countries and are constantly changing. At this time, there are three main types of rug-tufting guns:

- **CUT-PILE MACHINE**. It has a little pair of scissors that cuts each loop of yarn, leaving you with a soft, straight shag.

- **LOOP-PILE MACHINE**. This one doesn't have scissors, and it will leave you with a looped pile that is firmer and more compact than a cut pile.

- **PNEUMATIC MACHINE**. This can create both cut and loop shags, and it requires an air compressor. This gun is for advanced rug tufters.

For the projects in this book, we'll use a cut-pile tufting gun, which is the easiest to master. For more details on the tufting gun, see Getting to Know Your Tufting Gun on page 18.

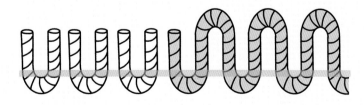

Cut-pile   Loop-pile

4. YARN

There are lots of types of yarn that you can use on your rug, and it all really comes down to preference. I use a super-high-quality acrylic yarn that I buy in Korea, but you don't have to go that far to find something good to work with. The thing I like about acrylic is that it's very soft and the colors pop, but it can get kind of dusty when you're working with it. Acrylic doesn't wear very well, so I use it mostly for art pieces and low-traffic areas. If you plan on placing your rug on the floor in a high-traffic area, you might want to go for a more durable material, such as wool, a wool blend, or even nylon, keeping in mind that what you gain in durability you sacrifice in cushy goodness. I also like to buy yarn that is already on a cone, but you can put literally any yarn onto a cone with a yarn winder.

For rug tufting, I like to use yarn with a 3–4 mm (.11–.14 in.) gauge. If you choose to use thinner yarn, you will need to use many strands at once. As for thicker yarn, the golden rule is: If it fits in the needle hole of your tufting gun, it will work. Otherwise, it's best to skip it.

5. YARN WINDER

If you plan to buy yarn that's not on a cone or wound into a cake, you may want to invest in a yarn winder. Winding your yarn will make it easier to work with and less likely to tangle while you're tufting.

6. YARN THREADER

A yarn threader will make threading your tufting gun a lot easier. Classic tufting gun threaders—long, looped wires with a plastic handle—break easily, and I don't like to use them. Instead, I use a metal crochet beading needle. It has a tiny hook on the end that works perfectly to thread yarn. Plus, you can poke it directly into your tufting cloth so that it's handy when you need to rethread. Crochet beading needles are skinny and easy to lose, and I glued a little black ball of black wire onto mine so that I can see it more easily. I suggest doing something similar with yours. If you don't have wire, gluing a short piece of brightly colored ribbon to your threader could work well, too.

7. FINAL BACKING FABRIC

I put final backing fabric on all of my pieces, whether I plan to hang them on a wall or place them on the floor. I like to think of it as sealing the rug. Also, the backing makes the piece look finished and beautiful. I find that felt with a non-slip pad on one side is the most versatile fabric. When you back your rug, you'll want the fabric to be larger than the rug itself—4–5 in. (10–13 cm) all around—which you will eventually cut back while fine-tuning the details of your rug.

8. GLUE

Glue is very important in rug tufting. Without it, the yarn will pop out of the tufting cloth and your rug will fall apart. You'll be spreading multiple layers of glue across the back of your rugs, so you'll need quite a bit. I suggest using latex glue that is meant for gluing tufted rugs. It adheres to yarn nicely, remains flexible when it dries, and is less toxic than other types of adhesives. You can find latex glue in craft stores and in larger sizes on websites such as Etsy.

While I believe latex glue is the best option, if it's not readily available, you can try using white school glue. Keep in mind that school glue will dry somewhat stiff, and it can become crumbly as time goes on. Some rug tufters also use Roberts, which is a brand of industrial carpet adhesive. Although Roberts adheres well and is flexible when dry, I don't recommend using this product due to off-gassing and toxicity.

9. SPATULA

A basic painting spatula will help you spread glue evenly on the back of your rug. A 3-in. (8-cm)–wide spatula with a little give will work great for the projects in this book. However, you can use any similar tool to spread the glue.

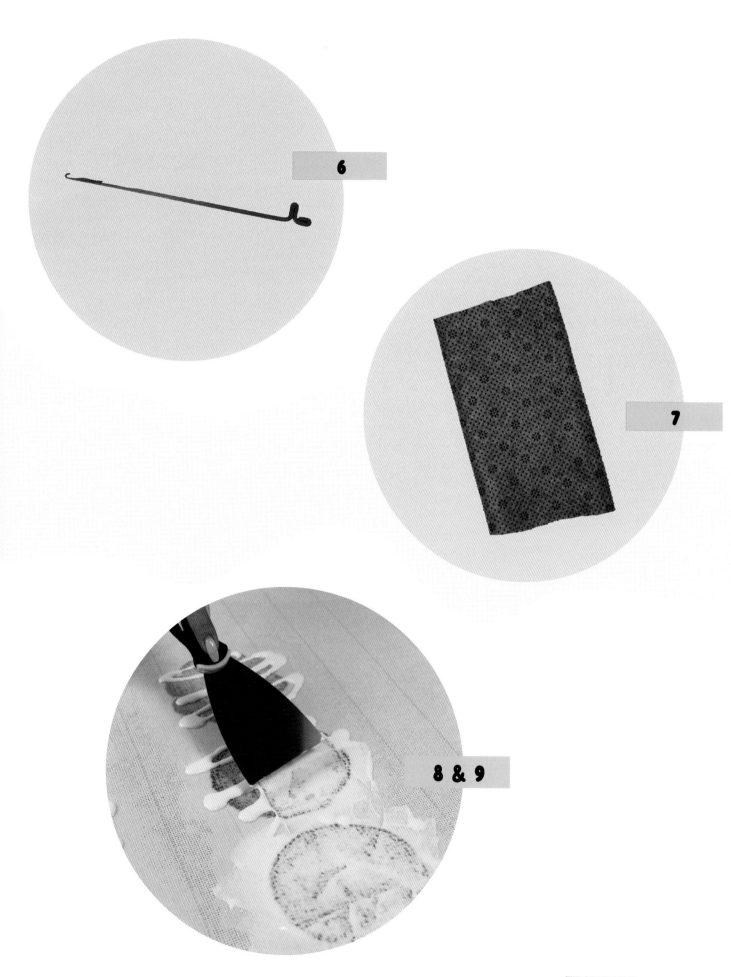

6

7

8 & 9

10. MESH (A.K.A. TULLE)

I am very excited to share this insider tip with you guys! I use mesh as part of a secondary gluing step. I learned this technique from master rug makers in South Korea, who have been creating beautiful works of art for generations. Adding mesh makes the back of the rug very pleasant and flat, preparing it for the final backing fabric, adding durability, and contributing to an overall nicer finish.

10

11 .SCISSORS & UTILITY KNIFE

We'll be snipping tufting cloth and other fabric, cutting rugs off the frame, carving clean lines between colors, and other fine work. So, a sharp pair of stainless-steel fabric scissors is essential. For me, an 8 in. (20 cm) pair works for pretty much everything. They come in different sizes, so choose a pair that feels comfortable in your hands. I also sometimes use a utility knife to cut rugs off the frame.

At the start of my tufting journey, I used child-safe craft scissors, and they were really hard on the hands. Now, I use Gingher scissors, which are specifically made for textiles, and they cut like butter! TOTAL GAME CHANGER!!!

12. CARPET SHAVER

I like to use a carpet shaver as part of my finishing process. It makes the shag uniform without taking away from the plushiness, and it really cleans up the look of the rug. It can also be used to carve clean lines between colors, if needed. Fun fact: I put cute googly eyes on it, so it looks like it's eating the fabric I'm shaving.

12

13. MARKER & PROJECTOR

If I'm not drawing a design freehand, I'll project my image onto stretched tufting cloth and trace it. The projects in this book will use projected images, so you'll need a projector unless you want to freeehand the designs! You don't have to buy anything fancy. In fact, my projector is very basic and doesn't have zooming capabilities like some fancy projectors out there. I just move it closer or further away from my tufting frame, depending on the size of rug I want to make. Look for a simple projector that you can connect to your phone or tablet and that has decent resolution so that the image will appear crisp and clear on your tufting cloth. Also, pick up a marker, like a Sharpie, so that you can trace the design.

14. DEVICE & ADAPTER CABLE

You'll be downloading the designs in this book onto a cell phone or laptop. You'll also need an adapter cable that can connect your phone, tablet, or laptop to the projector so that you can project each template onto your canvas.

15. OTHER TOOLS & MATERIALS

Here are a few more items you'll want to keep on hand when you start on your tufting journey.

- **FACE MASK**: Wearing a face mask, such as the N95 or KF94, is always a good idea as it offers some protection against floating yarn particles.

- **LINT ROLLER**: Using a lint roller will remove the smaller particles of yarn and dust from your rug and make the colors pop.

- **OIL & CLEANING BRUSH**: Your tufting gun works best when it is clean and lubricated. Applying a small amount of sewing oil or WD-40 to the parts that move, and then brushing with a small soft brush, will keep your tufting gun happy. However, try not to oil the needle or scissors directly, as the oil could transfer onto your rugs and make them dirty. If you do, just make sure to wipe it down well!

- **TWEEZERS**: You may need a pair of tweezers to fix mistakes and to push yarn fibers into place as a part of the finishing process.

- **VACUUM CLEANER**: You'll want a handheld vacuum cleaner to vacuum up all the dust that rug tufting will inevitably create. I like the ones that have a rotating brush attachment. I also have one without a brush to suck up the extra-clumpy yarn fluff—especially for after I shave a rug. But really, you can use whatever you have at home.

GETTING STARTED

Rug tufting is a simple process, and, with practice, your technique can improve greatly in a very short amount of time. But you can't just wield a power tool and make an amazing rug without knowing what to do, right? Here's the part where you figure out what you're working with and how to work it safely.

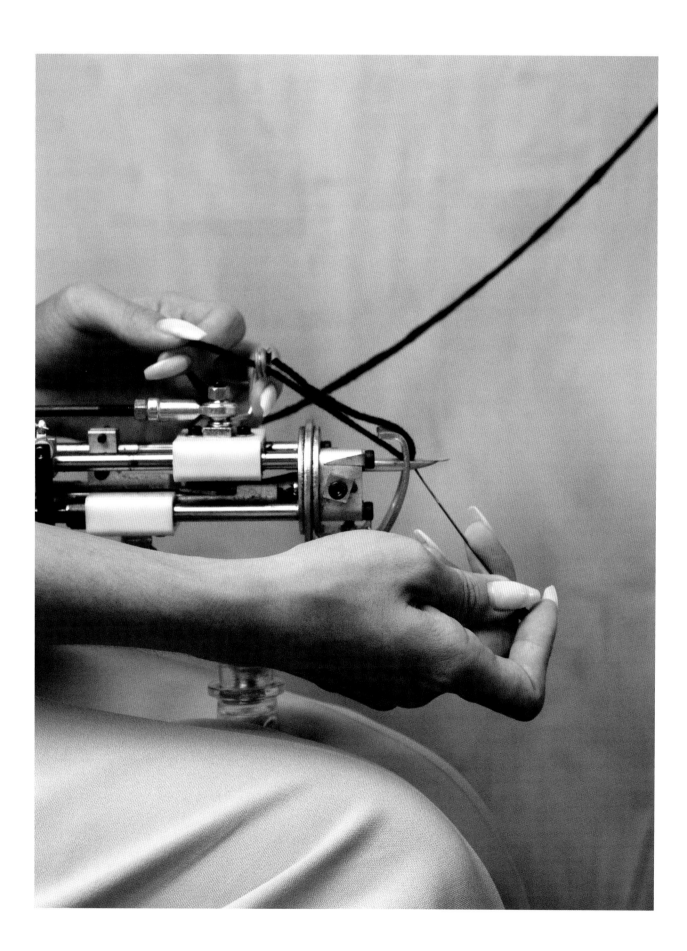

GETTING TO KNOW YOUR TUFTING GUN

So, you want to know how a tufting gun works? Of course! Here are the basic parts of a cut-pile machine. Check your owner's manual for details on your specific tufting gun.

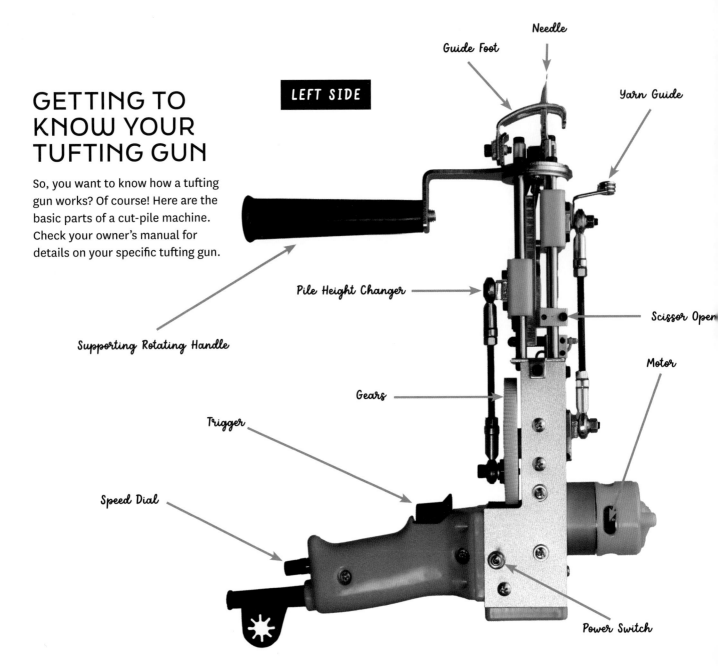

LEFT SIDE

Needle

Guide Foot

Yarn Guide

Pile Height Changer

Scissor Open

Motor

Supporting Rotating Handle

Gears

Trigger

Speed Dial

Power Switch

Say Hi to Your New Bestie

1. **POWER SWITCH**: Flip this switch to turn your tufting gun on and off.

2. **POWER INDICATOR LIGHT**: If this little light is lit, that means the power is on.

3. **TRIGGER**: The trigger starts and stops the tufting gun. Press and hold the trigger to begin tufting. Release the trigger to stop.

4. **SPEED DIAL**: This controls how fast the machine goes. For many tufting guns, level 1 is the slowest and level 8 is the fastest.

5. **MASTER SPEED SCREW**: This regulates the levels of the speed dial. If the slowest setting still feels too fast, use a screwdriver to adjust the speed screw to make it a little slower. You can also adjust the speed screw to make the fastest setting a little faster, but I don't recommend doing that if you're a beginner.

6. **ROTATING HANDLE**: Use the handle to support the front end of your tufting gun.

7. **NEEDLE**: This is where you thread your yarn. The needle punches the yarn in and out of the tufting cloth.

Rug Tufting with SIMJI

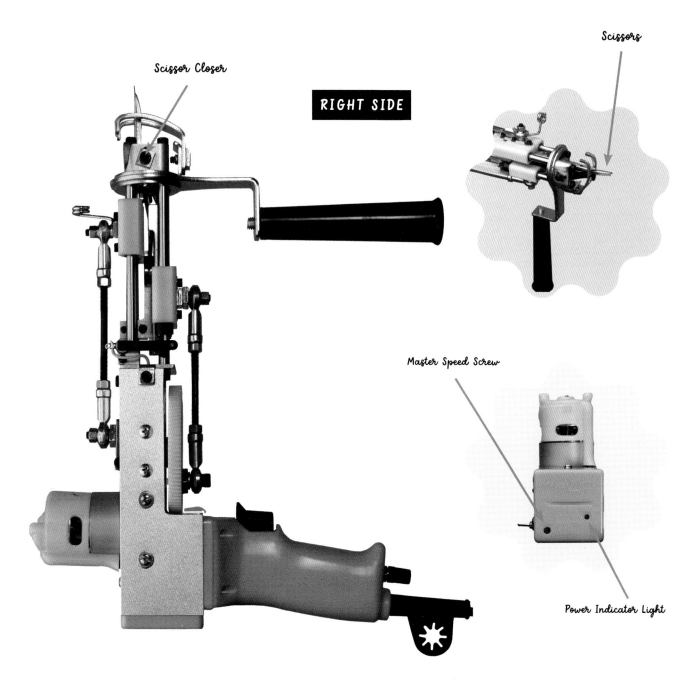

Scissor Closer

Scissors

RIGHT SIDE

Master Speed Screw

Power Indicator Light

8. **YARN GUIDE**: Feed the yarn through this little circle before threading it through the needle. Otherwise, the yarn could get caught in the moving parts of your tufting gun.

9. **GUIDE FEET**: The feet press against the fabric and help make your weave straight and even.

10. **SCISSORS**: The scissors push a loop of yarn through the needle and fabric, and then snip the end to make the end of the rug shaggy.

11. **PILE HEIGHT CHANGER**: This screw adjusts how long or short the pile of your rug will be. Loosen the screw to change the position of your scissors, which determines your pile height.

12. **GEARS**: These parts move the needle and the scissors.

13. **MOTOR**: The motor controls the gears.

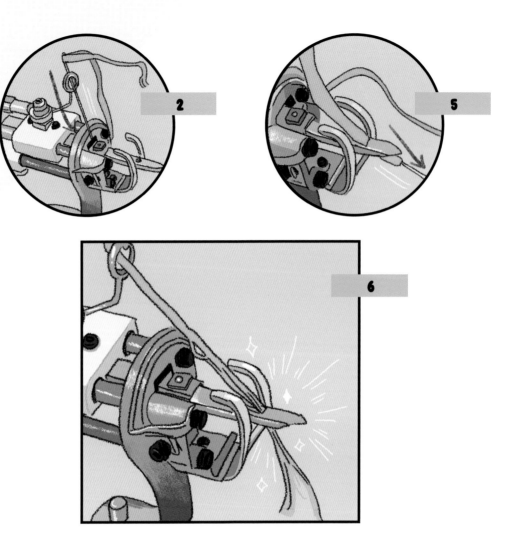

Here's How to Thread Your Machine

STEP 1: Make sure the tufting gun is in the off position. Sitting on a stool or in a chair, place the tufting gun securely on your lap with the needle facing away from you.

STEP 2: Push your yarn threader about halfway through the machine's yarn guide, toward you, hook side first.

STEP 3: Remove the threader from the yarn, and then hold on to the loop with one hand.

STEP 4: With your other hand, guide the threader underneath the needle and push it partially through the needle hole, hook side first.

STEP 5: Hook the loop of yarn onto the threader. Then carefully pull the threader and yarn back through the needle hole.

STEP 6: Pull the yarn back so that it sticks about ½" (1.3 cm) out of the needle hole. And that's it!

Rug Tufting with SIMJI

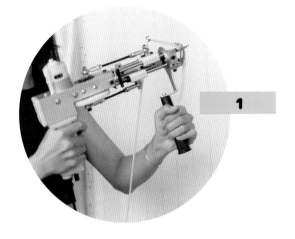

And Here's How to Work Your Machine

STEP 1: Holding the handle for support, pierce the needle into your stretched fabric until the feet of the tufting gun are firmly resting on the cloth.

STEP 2: Press the trigger and move the gun in an upward line at a pace that feels comfortable and controlled. This will activate the gears, making the scissors push loops of yarn through the fabric and snip the ends, leaving behind a cute shaggy rug on the opposite side.

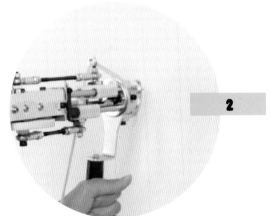

Safety Check

Learning how to use a rug-tufting gun is weird and maybe a little scary at first. Then, before you know it, the process becomes second nature. Of course, it goes without saying that you should use caution while operating a power tool with moving gears and sharp and snippy parts. Here are some other things to keep in mind before you begin rug tufting:

1. Rug tufting can cause loose yarn particles to float through the air. Choose a well-ventilated workspace or consider wearing a mask to keep your lungs safe. Using an air purifier is also an option. Vacuum your space often.

2. Always make sure that your tufting gun is turned *off* before you thread it. The threading process puts your hands in front of the needle and scissors, and you can cause some serious damage if you accidentally press the trigger.

3. Along the same lines, never put your hand in front of the gun or touch the gears when it is on. And make sure that no one is touching the backside of your canvas while you're working. It's dangerous.

4. Watch out for long hair or loose clothing, such as a hoodie string, which can get caught in the gears of the machine. If you can, tie back your hair and wear clothes that aren't too loose or drapey.

5. Working with a tufting gun is super fun, but it's definitely not a toy. Seriously. Respect the power tool and use it properly so that you don't get hurt.

TIPS & TECHNIQUES

Here, you'll find the most important tips and techniques that I've gathered throughout my tufting journey so far. I personally use them for each and every tufted rug I create. Follow these core principles throughout the projects in this book to create tufted cuteness as a confident beginner, and you'll find that these techniques will also carry you toward the next level of tufting and beyond. I've provided QR codes to videos in case you want to see these techniques in action!

SETTING UP YOUR TUFTING AREA

Choose a workspace that has lots of light and enough room to accommodate all of your tufting tools and materials. Since tufting is a dusty art and you'll be using adhesives, you'll want to be in a place that has good ventilation. Try to avoid carpeting as it can trap yarn fibers and be difficult to clean.

Once you've been tufting for a while, you might want to invest in yarn organizer pegs or shelving to keep your yarn collection sorted and to store your tools and other materials when you're not using them.

STRETCHING FABRIC

The key to a professional-looking rug begins with a good stretch. I learned this technique a few months after I started from a tufting master in South Korea, and it was a game changer. It gives me a near perfect stretch every time. Open your tufting fabric and gently drape it over the top of the frame. Leave about 3 in. (7.6 cm) of overhang on the top and left side of the frame. Cut the bulk of the fabric off the right side of the frame, leaving about 3 in. (7.6 cm) of overhang there, too. Leave the bottom as is for now.

To achieve a super straight stretch, we'll first remove a horizontal thread from the weave. I use a knitting needle to get underneath a stitch, and then wiggle it to loosen the thread. If you don't have a knitting needle, you can use a threading needle or something else that will allow you to get underneath the stitch. Next, tug at the loosened thread until you've pulled the entire thread out. This creates a long blank line across the top of the canvas that you can use as a guide since it is guaranteed to be straight. Hook the top left corner nail into your guideline. Tightly stretch the top of the fabric and hook the top right corner nail into the guideline. Next remove a vertical thread from the weave, where the top left nail is hooked, the same way you removed the horizontal thread. If the fabric bunches up while removing the thread, just pull the fabric back down into place. Once you have your vertical guideline, tightly stretch the fabric and hook the lower left corner nail into the guideline. Remove a vertical thread on the right side to create a guideline. Then tightly stretch the fabric down and to the right, and hook the bottom right corner nail into the guideline.

Carefully insert the remaining nails on the tufting frame into the top, left, and right guidelines, making sure that the fabric is securely affixed at the base of each nail. The fabric will stretch tighter with each side you affix. Once you've completed the three sides, gather the fabric at the bottom of the tufting frame, almost as if you are creating a cradle for your hand. Press your hand firmly into the cradle and stretch down the fabric as tightly as you can and gently push the stretched fabric into the tufting frame so that the nails hook onto it. Repeat until the bottom of the frame is lined with stretched fabric. Flick your finger onto the center of the fabric to test if it's tight enough. If it bounces back easily and sounds like a drum, you're good to go. If not, stretch the fabric at the bottom tighter. Cut off the excess fabric at the bottom of your frame, if desired.

How to Stretch
Your Fabric

What Makes a
Good Stretch?

What If the Stretch
Is Still Bad?

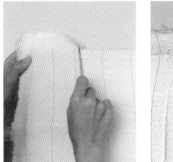  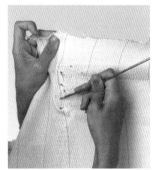

PROJECTING

If you don't want to freehand your designs, you'll want to use a projector to project your design onto the stretched tufting cloth. I like to put mine onto a tripod so I can easily adjust it as necessary. To ensure your rug looks like your design, you need to first flip it horizontally because the fluffy part will be on the back of the stretched fabric. Next, connect your device (laptop, tablet) and projector using an adapter cable. If you have a design that is white, remember to add a background color so you can see the design properly. To adjust the size of the rug, you can move your projector forward or back or zoom in or out on your design. Once you have your estimated size, focus your design so that it has sharp and clear lines—so satisfying! The keystone adjustment helps you make further tweaks to keep the design straight. If you need the rug to be a specific size, use a measuring tape on the projected image to check the size and adjust accordingly.

TRACING

I like to start by tracing the details first. I also tuft beginning with the details. I trace with a black marker and trace on the inside of the smallest details first moving outward with my design. If you have a really complex design, it's helpful to add a letter to represent each color right onto the design. Don't worry, the yarn will cover it up! Be careful not to move the projector as it is very hard to get it back to the correct position. Before you turn off the projector, cover it to make sure you traced everything correctly. Then turn on the lights and turn off the projector!

HOW TO HOLD A TUFTING GUN

Start by holding the back or butt end of the tufting gun with your dominant hand and using your non-dominant hand to hold the rotating handle. You'll steer the tufting gun with your dominant hand, not your support hand. The machine tufts up; you'll end up ripping the fabric if you try to tuft down. Wherever you move the butt end is the direction the machine will tuft, and the needle should always be pointing up.

VERTICAL & HORIZONTAL DENSITY

Depending on how dense you want each tufting line, you can hold back as you tuft up to create more vertical density. The space between each row of tufting determines how much horizontal density your tuft. I tend to like tufting a medium vertical density and every two holes of horizontal density. You'll get lots more practice tufting throughout the book but be sure to start with the Red Carpet warm-up rug!

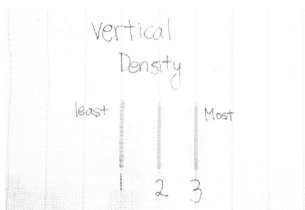

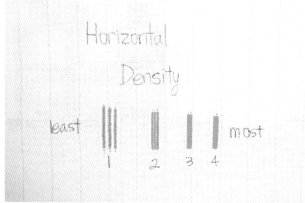

GLUING

Gluing the rug is a two-step process. You want to glue the rug while it is still on the frame so that the yarn doesn't unravel. First, you'll cover the back of the rug with a generous amount of latex glue, using a spatula to spread it evenly beyond the borders of the rug to make sure the sides are glued. Start with less glue because you can always add more. Then you'll add tulle or mesh that is larger than the rug and glue down the edges. This will stop the mesh from moving around. Add more glue to the entire rug and spread it evenly with a spatula. Let it dry for 24 hours or until dry. You can make it dry faster with a fan.

BACKING

Pour glue directly onto the back of your rug after the mesh layer has dried and gently spread the glue with your spatula so that it covers the rug, plus about 1" (2.5 cm) around the outside of the rug. Use as much glue as you need to cover the yarn well. Remember not to scrape the glue off with your spatula. Cut your backing fabric to size, which should be cut 2"–4" (5.1–10.2 cm) larger than your rug and center it on top with the non-slip side facing up. Press down on the fabric to make sure there are no wrinkles and press along the edges for a good hold. Let dry for 24 hours or until fully dry.

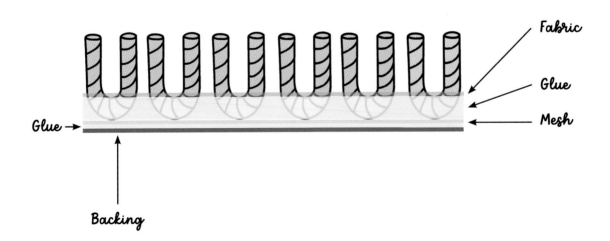

CUTTING OFF

Cut your completed and backed rug off the frame with extra space around it. Pull the yarn away to clearly see where you're cutting. Cut about 2 weaves away from the rug. If you pull the yarn away, you'll be able to see a little bit of the excess fabric but the yarn will cover it. That way you're sure not to cut into the rug by mistake! If you do end up cutting into the rug by mistake, just put a little glue on the part you cut into, no worries! You won't be able to tell from the front.

SHAVING

I personally like a cleaner tufted look so I opt to shave my rugs. Shaving creates a lot of yarn dust, so be sure to wear a mask. The goal is to even out the surface so glide the shaver along the top of the rug. Start slowly, you can always shave more but you can't add it back. Vacuum as you go. You can then take scissors and clean up the sides of the rug. I start first by brushing the yarn out to the sides and then clipping those fibers, then going back and beveling the yarn.

Tufting Tip

Note on Backing a Rug

SEPARATING COLORS

I have three main ways of doing this. The first option is to manually separate the two colors using a tool like a knitting needle. This works particularly well for straight lines. For designs that aren't straight lines you can move the colors using tweezers. Ceramic clay tools are also good options.

The second option is to carve with scissors. I cut between the two lines slightly angling my scissors beginning with one color and then switching to the other color.

The third option is to carve with a shaver. Wearing a mask, angle the shaver along one color side and then switch to the other side, vacuuming as you go. This creates a wider separation between the colors.

HOW TO PACK A RUG

I like to gift my rugs by rolling them and tying them closed with a beautiful ribbon or several strands of yarn that match the colors in the rug. Attaching a handwritten note to the rug with a sticker is always a nice touch.

If you're mailing your rug somewhere, I like to shrink-wrap the rug (using a heat gun) to protect it from any rain or humidity while shipping. And place it in a box filled with environmentally safe packing materials so that the rug stays safe and secure.

Separating with a knitting needle

Separating with scissors

Carving with a shaver

Top Ten Tips for Tufting Success

1. BE ORGANIZED. Lay out everything you need before you begin. Once you are finished, clean up your space and organize it for the next time. The more organized you are, the faster the process will be and the easier it will be to start your projects. Believe it or not, a neat and tidy space can inspire you!

2. LEARN HOW TO DEAL WITH THE DUST. Rug tufting is a dusty artform. When I first started, I was living in a studio apartment. Everything would be covered in dust—from my drying dishes to my clothes, and even my bed. Either work in a place that you are okay with being dusty or take precautions such as putting things in cabinets before you begin, covering furniture with cloth, and developing a personal relationship with your vacuum cleaner.

3. USE A GOOD, SOLID FRAME. A tight stretch is an essential foundation for a good rug, and a sturdy frame will help you achieve this. It's nearly impossible to get a tight stretch on a frame that is flimsy or doesn't grip your tufting cloth well.

4. HAVE A COMFORTABLE CHAIR. When you're sitting and tufting for hours, it can get really tiring and painful. When I first started, I sat on a wooden stool, and I was always in pain. Now, I have an ergonomic rolling chair that's padded, and my butt and back thank me.

5. REMEMBER TO STRETCH. Staying in one position for hours is not good for anybody. Get up and move around every once in a while—even if you are in the rug-tufting zone. Set a reminder on your phone if necessary.

6. ENRICH YOUR MIND WHILE YOU ARE TUFTING. Everything is just better with music, right? Also, listening to a podcast, current events, or even an audio book allows you to educate yourself while you are tufting. Embrace your inner multitasker!

7. DON'T BE AFRAID TO MESS UP. A lot of times mistakes will lead to "happy accidents" and force you to find a creative solution. In my experience, those accidents have led to some of my most inspired work.

8. BE CREATIVE. STAY INSPIRED. LET YOUR INNER CHILD RUN WILD! When it comes to creativity, there are no rules. Feel free to let loose and go wild. I provide you with templates and color suggestions in this book, but you don't have to follow my palettes at all. If you choose to, create your own. In fact, I encourage you to mix it up.

9. DO WHAT IS COMFORTABLE FOR YOU. After you've been tufting for a while, you may begin to discover your own process and techniques. That's awesome! You have to start somewhere to find your own way of doing things, and that's what this book is for.

10. TAKE THE THINGS THAT YOU LEARN HERE AND APPLY THEM TO YOUR OWN PROJECTS. Need I say more? Fly, my little bird. ☺

WARM UP: TUFT THE RED CARPET

Awhile back, I was invited to the Screen Actors Guild Awards and got to walk the red carpet. It was so exciting to see all my favorite actors and celebrities whose work I love and respect! I made a cute little red carpet to commemorate the experience, and I thought it would be a great simple warm-up for us to do here.

RED CARPET

TOOLS & MATERIALS

Tufting cloth	Spatula
Tufting frame	Scissors
Marker	Mesh
Ruler (optional)	Final backing fabric
Red yarn	Carpet shaver
Yarn threader	Vacuum
Tufting gun	Lint roller
Glue	

STEP 1: Stretch your tufting cloth onto the tufting frame.

STEP 2: Use a marker to draw a small rectangle, about 3" x 5" (7.6 x 13 cm). You can use a ruler or do it freehand like I did.

STEP 3: Set up your yarn by slipping it onto the yarn holder dowel on the frame. If you don't have a yarn holder, you can set the yarn on the floor. Thread a strand of red yarn onto the yarn-feeder loop near the top of your frame and pull the strand toward you.

STEP 4: Make sure that your tufting gun is turned off. Then thread the red yarn into the tufting gun.

4

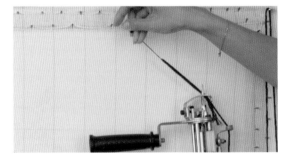

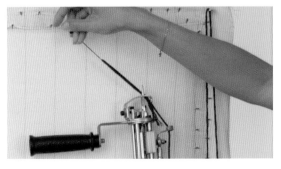

STEP 5: Let's begin by outlining the rug. Turn on your tufting gun and adjust it to the slowest setting. Hold the handle for support and pierce the needle into your stretched fabric, at the bottom right corner of the rug, just inside the line and until the feet of the tufting gun are firmly resting on the cloth. Press the trigger and move the gun from the bottom to the top of the line while applying medium pressure. When you reach the top, let go of the trigger. Now, turn your tufting gun to the left and tuft along the top of the rug from right to left. When you reach the end of the line, let go of the trigger. Bring your tufting gun to the bottom right corner of the rug, and tuft along the bottom line from right to left. Finally, tuft up the left side from bottom to top. Let go of the trigger once you complete the rectangle.

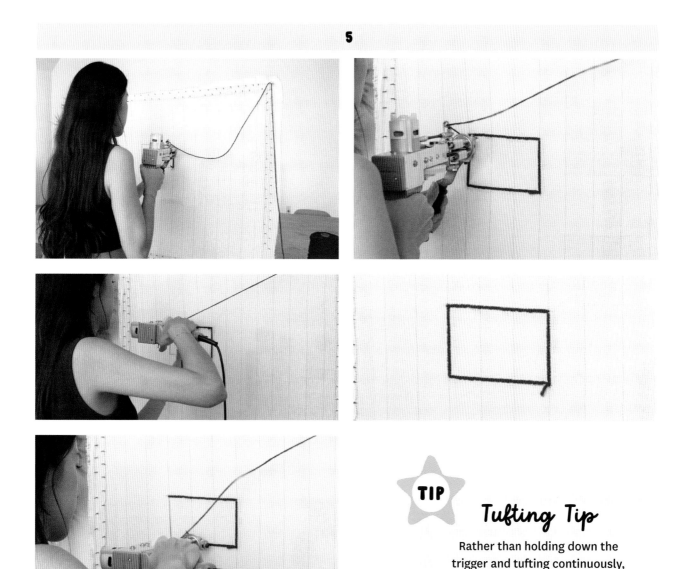

5

★ **TIP**

Tufting Tip

Rather than holding down the trigger and tufting continuously, you can also tuft by pulsing the trigger until you feel comfortable with the power of the machine.

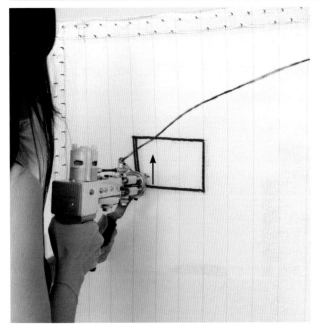
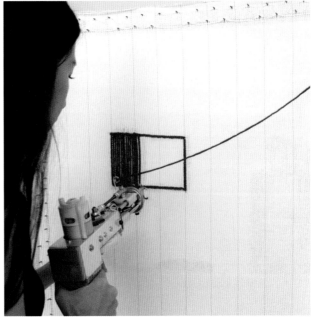

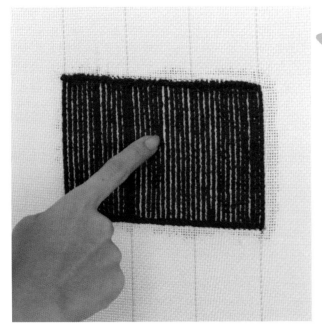

TIP

Tufting Tip

Be adaptable when you're tufting. Do you see hanging threads? Pull them out. One area seems a little too empty, fill it in, if you'd like. In the end, minor inconsistencies won't be noticed on the fluffy side of your rug.

STEP 6: Next we'll color in the rug. Starting at the left side of the rectangle, tuft a vertical line, from bottom to top. Then count two holes in the fabric and tuft another line from bottom to top. You can adjust to the density you desire. Repeat until the rug is completely filled in. When you reach the top of each line, let go of the trigger. Feel free to experiment with the tufting gun at different speeds to see how it feels or just keep it slow.

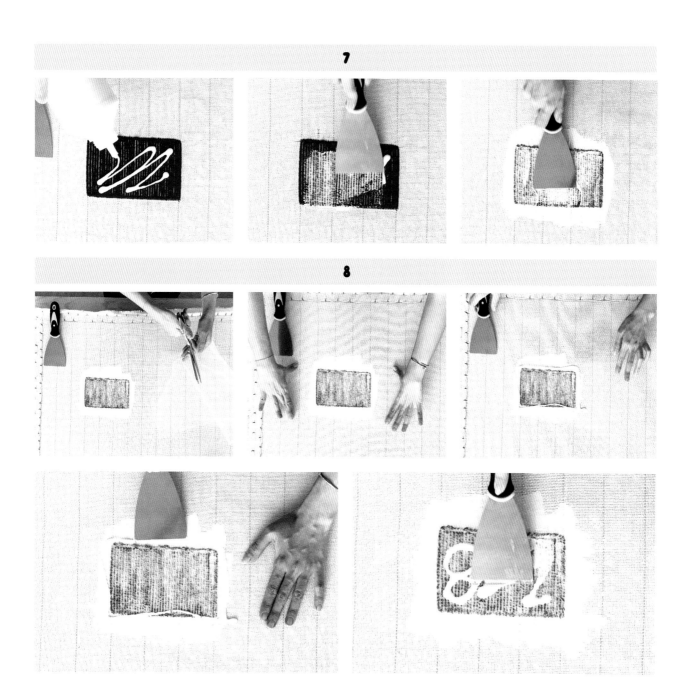

STEP 7: Quick clean-up time! Vacuum behind the frame and on the floor too, if you wish. Remove the clamps and place the frame on a table with the fluffy side down to prepare for gluing. Pour a generous amount of glue onto the rug. Use your spatula to evenly spread the glue. Extend the glue 1–2" (2.5–5.1 cm) past the edges. Use as much glue as you need to cover the rug thoroughly.

STEP 8: Grab your mesh and cut out a square that is about 2" (5.1 cm) larger than the edges of your red carpet. Lay the mesh on top of the red carpet. Pour glue on top of the mesh, near the edges of the rug. Use a spatula to gently spread the glue from the edge of the rug outward, securing the mesh to the tufting cloth. This keeps the mesh from moving around when you glue it down. Now pour glue over the entire rug and spread it around. Flatten any wrinkles with your spatula as you secure the mesh to the rug and the canvas. Let dry for 24 hours or until fully dry.

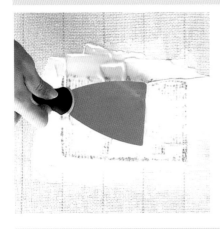
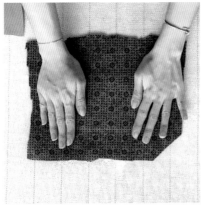

STEP 9: Cover the rug with another generous layer of glue. Spread it evenly with a spatula, making sure to extend the glue past the edges of the rug. Cut a piece of final backing fabric that is about 2" (5.1 cm) larger than the edges of your red carpet. Set aside. Cover the rug with the final backing fabric that you cut earlier, with the non-slip side up. Smooth the fabric and press down on the edges to secure it. Let dry for 24 hours or until fully dry.

STEP 10: Use scissors to cut the rug off the frame, leaving some excess tufting cloth around the rug. Flip over the rug so that the tufted part is on top. Carefully snip off excess tufting cloth, making sure not to snip into the rug itself. Hold back the tufted yarn and cut the cloth as close and as evenly as possible to the rug without cutting into it. For rectangle rugs, I like to angle the corners a bit so that they are not so spiky.

TIP

Tufting Tips

When applying glue, try not to scrape your spatula along the back of your rug. If you do, you'll end up removing glue and compromising the strength of your rug.

———

To speed the drying process, I bought a carpet dryer fan which really cuts down on the drying time!

STEP 11: If you like the scruffy look, you can leave the rug as is or if you like a cleaner, tidier look, like me, you can shave it. Wearing a mask, glide the shaver gently along the top of the rug to make it uniform. Vacuum the rug. Then snip the hanging yarn from around the edges. Angle your scissors as you cut around the edges to create a slightly rounded bevel that is neat and sculpted. Vacuum again. Roll a lint roller over the rug to get any last pieces of dust.

Congratulations, you just made your first tufted rug!

TIP

Tufting Tip

It's better to cut too little than too much at first. You can always cut more later if you need to. However, if you happen to cut into your rug, put a little latex glue on the area to keep the rug from unraveling.

PROJECTS

In this section, I'll show you how to make ten of the cutest rugs ever. Rugs aren't just for the floor, and there's something for every mood. If you're hungry for something cute and practical, you'll love the Fuzzy Burger Coaster Set. We'll surround ourselves with citrus by making the Orange You Glad Mirror Rug. We'll add fun to our fits with Thrift Lift Rug Patches, Two-Toned Mini Tote and create the cutest home décor with the Forever Flower Rug!

After each tufting project, you'll find a bonus rug project to make, which will allow you to practice similar principles, improve your skills, and express your own personal flair.

Are you ready to get started? Let's goooooooooo!

FUZZY BURGER COASTER SET

I love surprising friends and family with unexpected cuteness. This six-piece stack-able Fuzzy Burger Coaster Set protects furniture *and* makes guests smile.

Size: 4¼"–4½" (10.8–11.4 cm), depending on the size of cups or mugs you want to use

TOOLS & MATERIALS

Tufting cloth

Tufting frame

Fuzzy Burger Coaster Set template

Cell phone, tablet, or laptop

Projector

Adapter cable that can connect the projector to your device

Marker

Yarn (colors: dark brown, brown, cream, salmon, classic red, light green, green, tan, and yellow)

Yarn threader

Tufting gun

Vacuum

Glue

Spatula

Scissors

Mesh

Final backing fabric

Utility knife (optional)

Carpet shaver

Lint roller

Tweezers

1

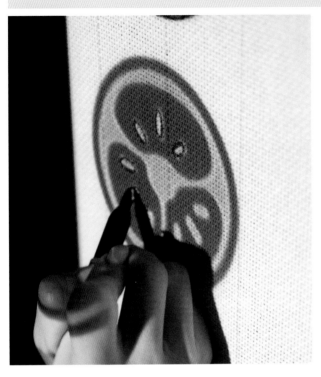

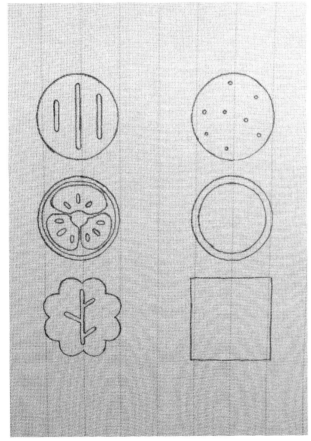

STEP 1: Stretch your tufting cloth onto the tufting frame and download the Fuzzy Burger Coaster Set template. Remember to flip the image horizontally! Adjust the size of the projected image so that the bottom of a cup or mug will comfortably fit on the coasters, and make sure the image is level. Use a marker to trace the images, beginning with the details then moving on to the outlines. Turn on your lights to check your work before you move the projector.

TIP

Tufting Tip

For small rugs, rather than centering the template on your canvas, try projecting the image toward a left or right corner, making sure to steer clear of nails of the frame. This way, you could make another small rug with the empty space on the stretched cloth.

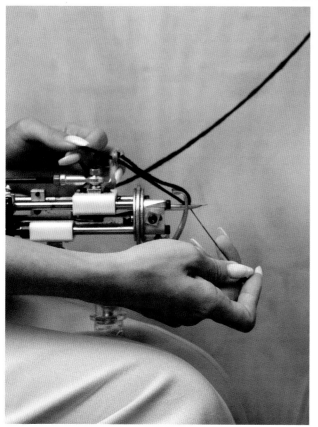
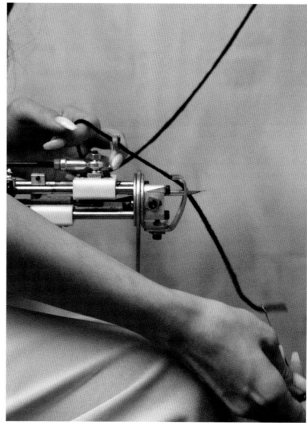

TIP

Tufting Tip

If you're designing a multi-piece rug like this coaster set, put all of your pieces onto one template so that you can easily maintain the correct proportions of each rug.

STEP 2: Let's begin with the dark brown grill marks on the burger patty. Set up your yarn by slipping it onto the yarn holder dowel on the frame. If you don't have a yarn holder, you can set the yarn on the floor. Thread a strand of dark brown yarn onto the yarn-feeder loop near the top of your frame and pull the strand toward you. Make sure that your tufting gun is turned off. Then thread the dark brown yarn into the tufting gun.

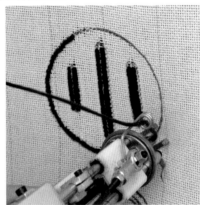

STEP 3: Turn on your tufting gun and adjust it to the slowest setting. Hold the handle for support and pierce the needle into your stretched fabric, at the bottom of the first grill mark, until the feet of the tufting gun are firmly resting on the cloth. Press the trigger and allow the gun to glide from the bottom to the top of the grill mark while applying medium pressure. Repeat until the first grill mark is filled. Do the same for the other two grill lines.

STEP 4: Now, let's outline the patty. Replace the yarn on the dowel with the regular brown yarn. Rethread your tufting gun with the new yarn. Pierce the tufting gun needle into the bottom center of the circle, just inside the line. Tuft up the left side of the circle until you reach the top center. Then go back to the bottom center and tuft up the right to complete the circle.

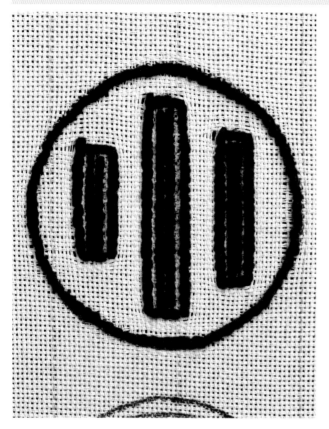

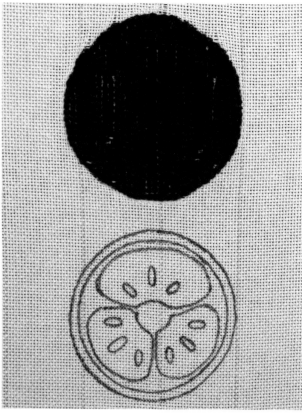

6

STEP 5: Next, outline the grill marks with brown. Then fill in the patty. Starting at the left side of the circle, tuft vertical lines, from bottom to top, until the patty is completely filled in.

STEP 6: Moving on to the tomato! Replace the yarn on the dowel with the cream-colored yarn, which we'll use for the seeds. You'll see in the image that I used a salmon-colored yarn at first, but it didn't show up well enough so I switched to cream. Rethread your tufting gun with the new yarn. Make sure your tufting gun is set to the slowest setting. Pick a seed and start at its bottom left. Pulse and push your gun forward until you reach the top of the seed. Go back to the bottom and move your gun up the right side of the seed. Hold back on the gun as you tuft this small area so it is denser. Do this for all of the seeds. Don't worry about being perfect. In fact, remember this motto: Imperfect equals charming!

TIP

Tufting Tip

This is a good point in the book to remind ourselves that we can change our design mid-project,
if we want to. Also, you don't have to use the same colors that I do, if you don't want to!
You'll notice that the pictures show me tufting salmon-colored seeds. However, after I finished the
tomato, I decided that the seeds would look better in a cream color. So, I carefully plucked out
the salmon-colored seeds with a pair of tweezers and retufted them in cream.
I love how it turned out!

Rug Tufting with SIMJI

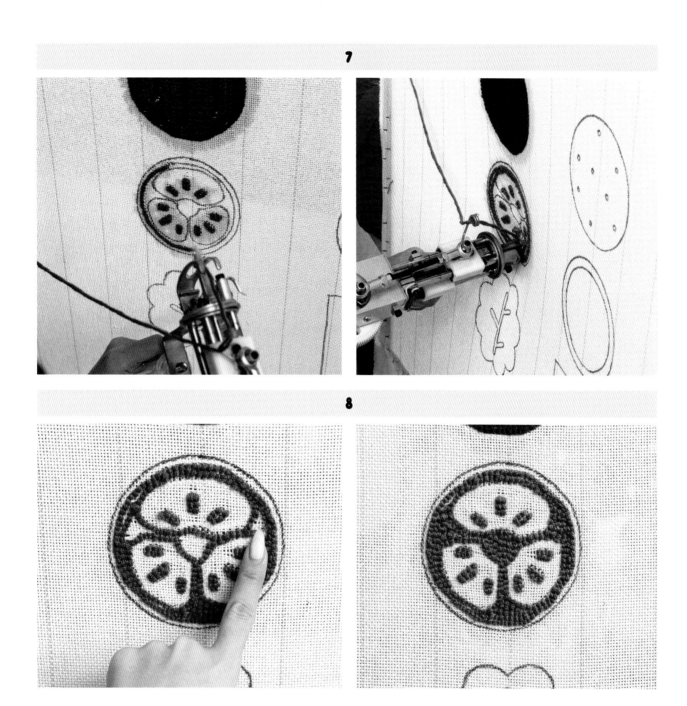

STEP 7: Replace the yarn on the dowel with salmon-colored yarn. Rethread your tufting gun with the new yarn. Outline the inner circle that goes around the three curvy shapes around the seeds. Then, outline the three curvy shapes themselves.

STEP 8: Fill in the gaps between the curvy shapes. These areas are tight, so you may have to tuft horizontally or at an angle to get into the crevices. Finally, tuft the circle at the center of the tomato with vertical lines.

STEP 9: Next, replace the yarn on the dowel with classic red yarn. Rethread your tufting gun with the new yarn. Outline the inside of the curvy shapes around the seeds, and then outline the seeds themselves.

STEP 10: Fill in the gaps between the seeds and the curvy shapes. Again, these areas are tight. You may have to adjust your body to tuft at different angles to get into the crevices. Finally, tuft around the outer circle of the tomato. After I finished, I decided that the seeds would look better in a cream color (see below).

STEP 11: Now, it's time to tuft the lettuce leaf. Replace the yarn on the dowel with the light green yarn. Rethread your tufting gun with the new yarn, and then tuft the veins in the center of the lettuce leaf.

FUZZY BURGER COAS

10

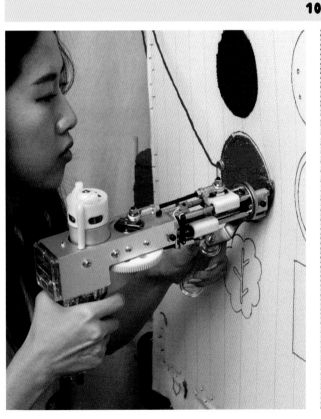

　　Rug Tufting with SIMJI

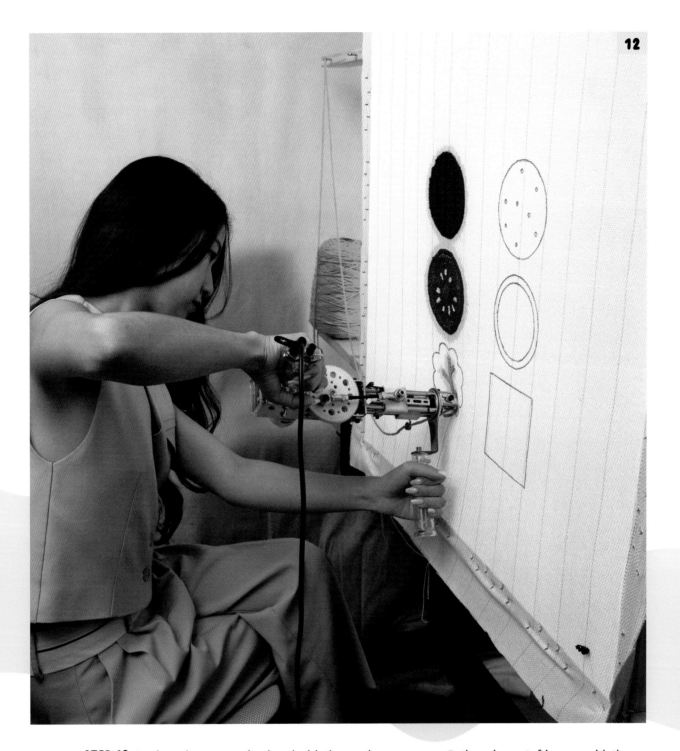

STEP 12: Replace the yarn on the dowel with the regular green yarn. Rethread your tufting gun with the new yarn. First, outline the light green veins in the center of the leaf. Then, outline the entire leaf. Start at the bottom center and tuft up the left side of the leaf until you reach the top center. Then, go back to the bottom center and tuft up the right side to complete the leaf.

Rug Tufting with SIMJI

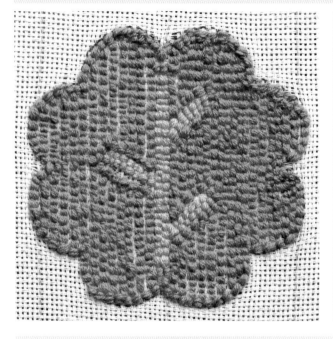

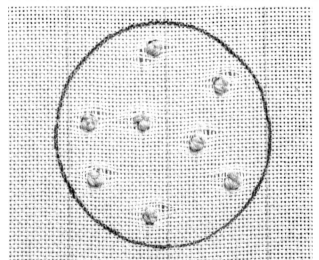
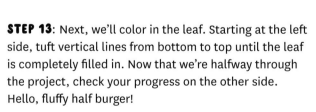

Front

STEP 13: Next, we'll color in the leaf. Starting at the left side, tuft vertical lines from bottom to top until the leaf is completely filled in. Now that we're halfway through the project, check your progress on the other side. Hello, fluffy half burger!

STEP 14: Let's move on to the bun pieces. The top and bottom of the bun use the same colors, so we'll do them at the same time. Replace the yarn on the dowel with the cream-colored yarn. Rethread your tufting gun with the new yarn. Holding the handle of your tufting gun for support, pierce the needle into the center of a seed on the top bun. The seeds are super tiny, so you'll need to pulse the trigger and twist the machine to tuft them holding back a bit. Use this technique to tuft all of the seeds on the top bun.

15

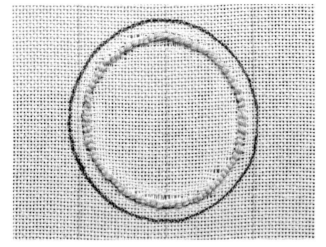
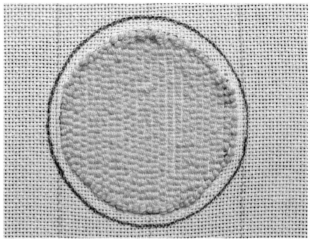

16

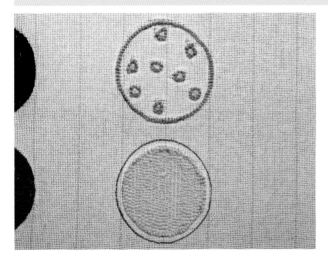
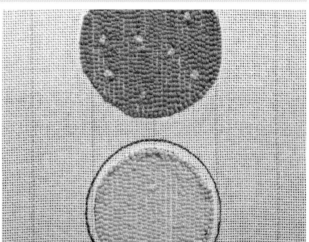

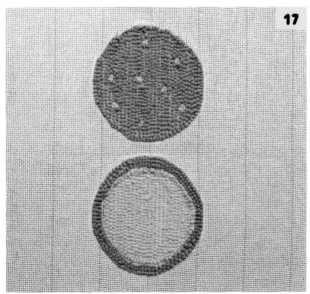

17

Rug Tufting with SIMJI

STEP 15: Using the same yarn, outline the inner circle of the bottom bun. Now, let's fill it in. Starting at the left side of the circle, tuft vertical lines, from bottom to top, until the area is completely filled in.

STEP 16: Replace the yarn on the dowel with tan yarn. Rethread your tufting gun with the new yarn. Outline the outer circle of the top bun, as well as the seeds. Then, beginning at the left side of the bun, tuft vertical lines from bottom to top until it is completely filled in.

STEP 17: Now, using the same tan yarn, outline the bottom bun. Begin at the bottom center of the bun and tuft up the left side. Go back to the bottom center and tuft up the right side. Since this is such a tight area, continue to use the outlining technique to fill in the rest of the bun.

STEP 18: Last but not least, let's color the cheese, which is a yellow square (or another color if you'd like a different type of cheese). Change the yarn on the dowel to yellow and rethread your tufting gun. Outline the square. Then, starting at the bottom left side, tuft vertical lines from bottom to top until the cheese is filled in. Check out the tufted side. How cute is that?

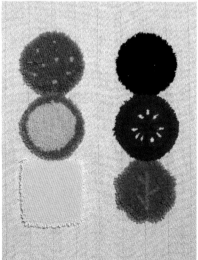

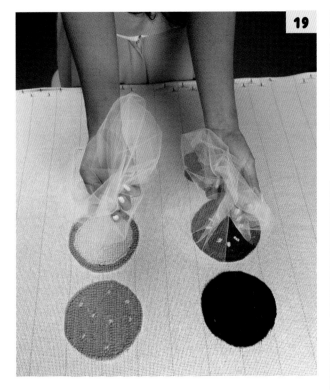

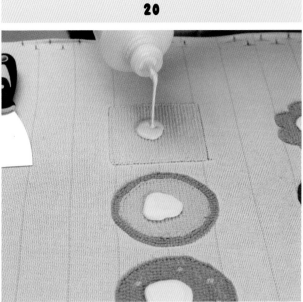

STEP 19: Vacuum the area behind the frame. Remove the clamps and place the frame on a table with the fluffy side down. Lay the mesh on top of your frame and cut one row of mesh for each row of the burger elements that is about 2" (5.1 cm) larger than the edges of each row. Cut two similar-size pieces of your final backing fabric for a later step. Set everything aside.

STEP 20: Pour a generous amount of glue onto each rug. Use your spatula to evenly spread the glue. Extend the glue 1"–2" (2.5–5.1 cm) past the edges of the yarn. Use as much glue as you need to cover the rug thoroughly.

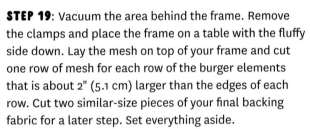

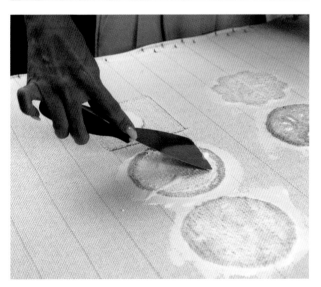

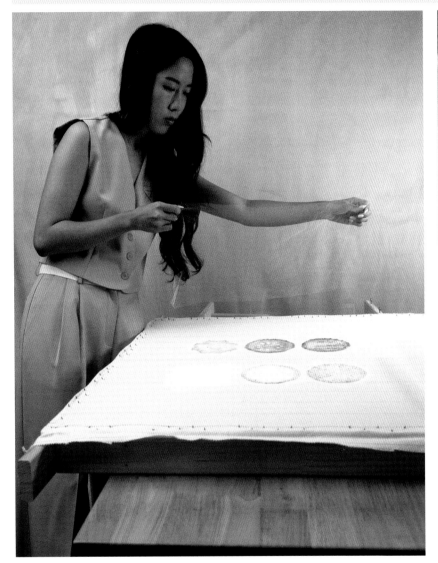

STEP 21: Lay the two rows of mesh on top of the burger elements. Pour glue on top of each row of mesh, near the edges of the rugs. Gently spread the glue from the edge of the rugs outward, securing the mesh to the canvas. Pour glue over the entire rug and spread it around. Flatten any wrinkles with your spatula as you secure the mesh to the rug and the canvas. Let dry for 24 hours or until dry.

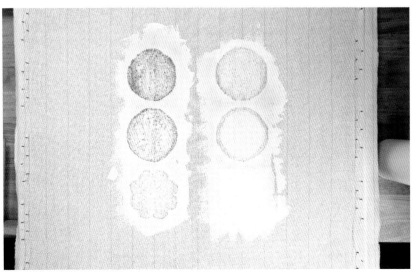

STEP 22: Once dry, cover the rugs with another generous layer of glue, making sure to extend the glue past the edges of the yarn. Cover each row with the final backing fabric that you cut earlier. Smooth the fabric and press down to secure it. Don't press down too hard, because the glue could seep through the fabric, but make sure that the edges of each coaster are securely adhered to the backing fabric so your rug stays together. Let dry for 24 hours or until dry.

 TIP

Tufting Tip

Test that the final backing fabric is completely dry by peeling it back and giving it a little tug. If the backing peels off or is tacky, the glue isn't dry enough. If it doesn't budge, you're good to go.

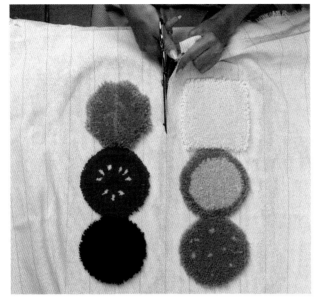

STEP 23: Carefully remove the rugs and tufting cloth from the frame. Flip over the rugs so that the tufted part is on top. So cute! Now, you'll be using scissors to carefully cut out each rug. Fold the tufting cloth in between each coaster to help you see where you should be cutting. Hold back the tufted yarn and carefully cut the cloth as close and as evenly as possible to the rugs without cutting into them.

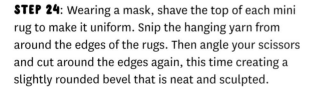

STEP 24: Wearing a mask, shave the top of each mini rug to make it uniform. Snip the hanging yarn from around the edges of the rugs. Then angle your scissors and cut around the edges again, this time creating a slightly rounded bevel that is neat and sculpted.

STEP 25: Vacuum each coaster. Roll a lint roller over it to make the colors pop. To create a really finished look, go in with tweezers and move individual yarn threads to ensure the lines between yarn colors are sharp. Assemble your burger. I did it this way: bottom bun, burger, cheese, tomato, lettuce, top bun. Yum!

TRY IT YOURSELF
JUICY FRUIT COASTER SET

Now that you know how to tuft the Fuzzy Burger Coaster Set, you're ready to use the same technique for all kinds of mini rugs. I've included another cute and yummy design. This one has mix-and-match shapes and details that are slightly harder than the burger. See the condensed step-by-step instructions, and have fun with it! You'll need all the same tools and materials as the Fuzzy Burger Coaster Set, but different yarn colors to match the fruit pieces.

YARN COLORS

Red

Black

White

Dark green

Dark orange

Regular orange

Light orange

Peach

Orange

Brown

White

Bright green

Avocado green

Bright yellow

Light yellow

STEP 1: Stretch your tufting cloth onto the tufting frame and download the Juicy Fruit Coaster Set template. Remember to flip the image horizontally! Project and adjust the size of the projected image so that the bottom of a cup or mug will comfortably fit on the coasters, and make sure the image is level. Use a marker to trace the images beginning with the details and working your way out. Check your work before you move the projector.

STEP 2: Begin with any piece of fruit you'd like. Start with the yarn for the smallest detail first. Put it on the yarn holder dowel on the frame or on the floor. Thread a strand of yarn onto the yarn-feeder loop near the top of your frame and pull the strand toward you. Make sure that your tufting gun is turned off and thread the yarn into the tufting gun. Tuft the selected small detail, then continue. Rethread your tufting gun with different colored yarn as necessary. For larger details, outline first, and then tuft vertical lines from bottom to top until the section is completely filled in. Do this for each piece of fruit.

STEP 3: Vacuum the area behind the frame. Remove the clamps and place the frame on a table with the fluffy side down. Lay the mesh on top of your frame and cut two rows of mesh that are about 2" (5.1 cm) larger than the edges of each row of coasters. Cut two similar-size pieces of your final backing fabric for a later step. Set everything aside.

STEP 4: Pour a generous amount of glue onto each rug. Use your spatula to evenly spread the glue. Extend the glue 1"–2" (2.5–5.1 cm) past the edges of the yarn. Use as much glue as you need to cover the rug thoroughly. Then lay the two rows of mesh on top of the fruit. Pour glue on top of the mesh, first taking it down to the outer edges, then pouring more onto the middle of the rugs. Gently spread the glue from the edge of the rugs outward, securing the mesh to the canvas. Let dry for 24 hours or until dry.

STEP 5: Once dry, cover the rugs with another generous layer of glue, making sure to extend the glue past the edges of the yarn. Cover each row with the final backing fabric that you cut earlier. Smooth the fabric and press down, making sure that the edges of each coaster are securely adhered to the backing fabric. Let dry for 24 hours or until dry.

STEP 6: Carefully remove the rugs and tufting cloth from the frame. Flip over the rugs so that the tufted part is on top. Carefully cut out each rug and then cut off any excess tufting cloth. Wearing a mask, shave the top of each mini rug to make it uniform. Snip the hanging yarn from around the edges of the rugs. Then, angle your scissors and cut around the edges again, this time creating a slightly rounded bevel that is neat and sculpted.

STEP 7: Vacuum each coaster rug. Roll a lint roller over it to make the colors pop and tweeze the individual threads to get clean lines. Stack your fruit coasters to display them until you're ready to use them!

ORANGE YOU GLAD MIRROR RUG

Have you ever seen those gigantic, orange-shaped foam hats with straps that attach under the chin? They're so bright and happy! I'm a fan of all things cheerful, and what's more cheerful than being surrounded by fruit? You'll definitely start the day bright when you gaze into this fluffy orange rug mirror. Vitamin C not included.

Size: 9" (22.9 cm) in diameter

TOOLS & MATERIALS

Tufting cloth

Tufting frame

Orange You Glad Mirror Rug template

Cell phone, tablet, or laptop

Projector

Adapter cable that can connect the projector to your device

Round mirror of desired size (I used an 8" [20.3 cm]-diameter mirror)

Marker

Yarn (colors: white, dark orange, green, and light orange)

Yarn threader

Tufting gun

Vacuum

Glue

Spatula

Scissors

Mesh

Final backing fabric

Utility knife (optional)

Carpet shaver

Glass cleaner and paper towel (optional)

Lint roller

Tweezers

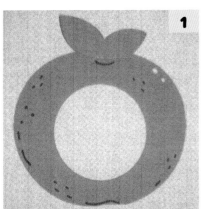

STEP 1: Stretch your tufting cloth onto the tufting frame, and download the Orange You Glad Mirror Rug template onto your cell phone, tablet, or laptop, and open the image. Flip the image horizontally. When you tuft, you will be working on the back side of the rug. Use an adapter cable to connect the projector to your device. Turn on the projector and point it toward your tufting frame so that the template appears on the cloth. Turn off the lights so that you can see the image clearly.

STEP 2: With the mirror's reflective side facing the tufting cloth, hold it in front of the white center of the template to check sizing. Adjust the size of the projected image so that the mirror is 1½"–2" (3.8–5.1 cm) larger than the white circle. This will ensure that the mirror attaches securely to the rug later. I used an 8" (20.3 cm) diameter mirror, but you can use whatever size you wish.

STEP 3: Use a marker to trace the image. Once you are finished tracing, check that everything is correct before moving the projector.

TIP

Tufting Tip

To fill tiny circles, hold the handle of your tufting gun for support and pierce the needle into the center of the small circle. Pulse the trigger, then twist the machine slightly counterclockwise (or clockwise, if it's more comfortable). Pulse again, and then twist slightly again in the same direction. Pulse and twist until you've filled the circle. The circles don't have to be perfect. If anything, it's cuter when they're not perfect.

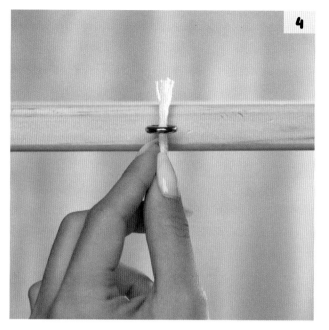

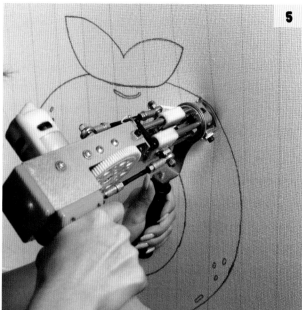

STEP 4: Let's start with the white details that give the orange some highlights, since we're using only a small amount of this color. Set up your yarn by slipping it onto the yarn holder dowel on the frame. If you don't have a yarn holder, you can set the yarn on the floor. Thread a strand of yarn onto the yarn-feeder loop near the top of your frame and pull the strand toward you. Make sure that your tufting gun is turned off. Then thread the yarn into the tufting gun.

STEP 5: Turn on your tufting gun and adjust it to the slowest setting. You'll be tufting in a tiny area, so you don't want to go too fast. Hold the handle for support and pierce the needle into your stretched fabric until the feet of the tufting gun are firmly resting on the cloth. Press the trigger and glide the gun in an upward line while applying medium pressure and holding back a bit to give the detail more density. Repeat until the area is filled. Do the same for the other white circle.

STEP 6: Next, we'll tackle the small details that give the orange some dimension. Replace the yarn on the dowel with dark orange yarn. Rethread your tufting gun with the new yarn. I'm using double yarn in my tufting gun because the yarn I have in this color is slightly thinner than the 3–4 mm (.11–.14") gauge I normally use. Whether you choose to use one strand or two, the technique for threading your tufting gun is the same. Repeat step 7 for the dark orange and you're done with the tiny details.

Rug Tufting with SIMJI

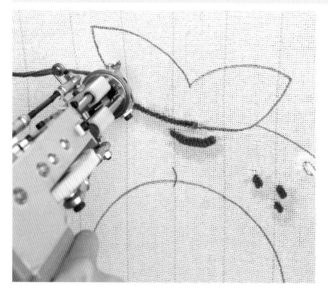

STEP 7: Now, let's outline the leaf. Replace the yarn on the dowel with green yarn. Rethread your tufting gun with the new yarn. Pierce the tufting gun needle into the bottom center of the leaf, just inside the line. Then tuft around the leaf.

STEP 8: Next, we'll color in the leaf. Starting at the left side, tuft vertical lines from bottom to top until the leaf is completely filled in. Once you've done that, check your progress on the other side. It still doesn't look like an orange yet, but that's a pretty cute leaf.

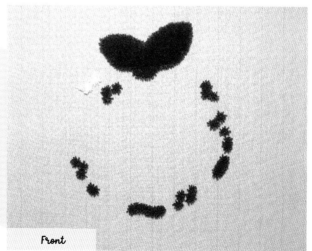

Front

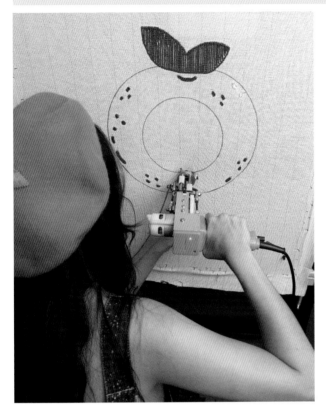

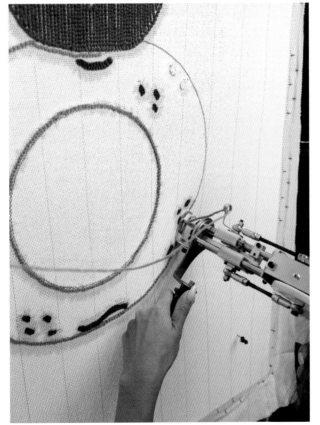

STEP 9: On to the last color. Replace the yarn on the dowel with light orange yarn. Rethread your tufting gun with the new yarn. To tuft the inner circle, start from the center bottom, then go up the left side to the top. Because you always have to tuft up, you can't go all the way around the circle. Instead, go back to the center bottom and tuft up the right side. Then tuft around the inside of the stem and use the same method to tuft around the outer circle.

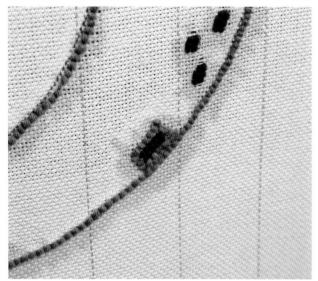

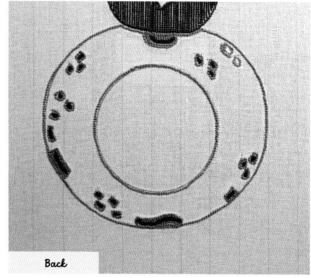

Back

Front

STEP 10: Tuft around the details inside the orange. Creating an outline of the details will ensure that your details look polished and make it easier to fill in the larger areas. Once you've done that, this is what it will look like on the other side!

 TIP

Tufting Tip

Don't worry if you see a straight strand of yarn sticking out at the bottom of a line of tufting. This strand is an extra piece of yarn, which is not tufted and is safe to pull out and discard. Tufted yarn will look like a V shape.

ORANGE YOU GLAD MIRROR RUG ORANGE YOU GLAD MIRRC

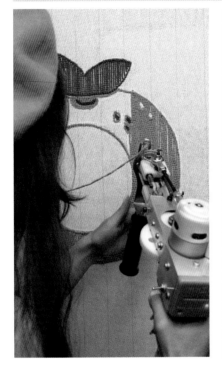

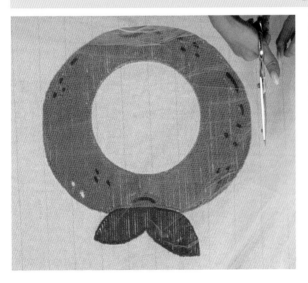

STEP 11: Now, it's time to fill in the center. Starting from one side of the orange, tuft vertical lines side by side and from bottom to top until the orange is completely filled. I went from right to left. You're done tufting! How cute is the fluffy side?

STEP 12: Vacuum the area behind the frame. Remove the clamps and place the frame on a table with the fluffy side down. Lay your mesh on top of the rug. Cut out a piece of mesh that is about 4" (10.2 cm) larger than the edges of your rug. Then cut a similar-size piece of your final backing fabric for a later step. Set both aside.

Rug Tufting with SIMJI

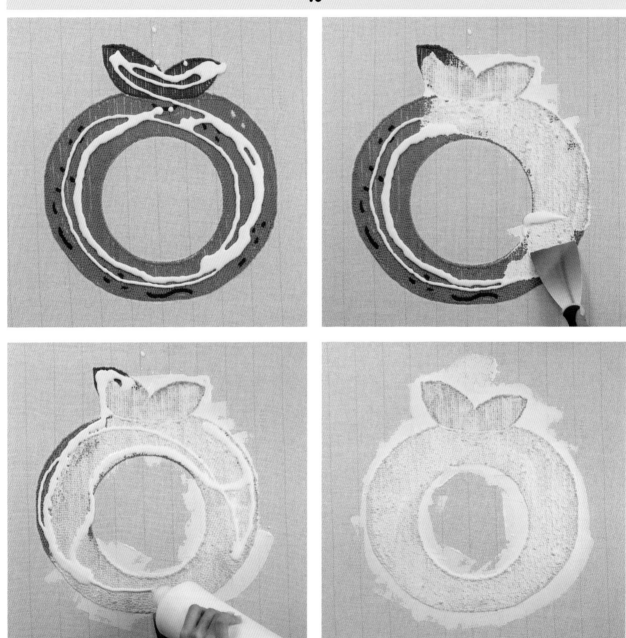

STEP 13: Pour a generous amount of glue onto your rug. Use your spatula to evenly spread the glue. Use as much glue as you need to cover the rug thoroughly.

ORANGE YOU GLAD MIRRO

Rug Tufting with SIMJI

STEP 14: Lay the mesh on top of the rug. Pour glue on top of the mesh, near the edges of the rug. Gently spread the glue from the edge of the rug outward, securing the mesh to the canvas. This keeps the mesh from moving around when you glue it down. Now, pour glue over the entire rug and spread it around. Flatten any wrinkles with your spatula as you secure the mesh to the rug and the canvas. Let dry for 24 hours or until dry.

G ORANGE YOU GLAD MIRROR RUG ORANGE YOU GLAD MIR

STEP 15: Use your scissors or a utility knife to remove the white center of your rug, taking care not to cut the tufted areas. Put the circle aside. Then, use your scissors to snip the edges of the tufting cloth to make them smooth.

STEP 16: It's time to attach the mirror. Line the center edge of the rug with glue and gently spread outward 3"–4" (7.6–10.2 cm). You want a generous layer of glue here. Place the mirror, reflective side down, over the center hole and onto the glue. Note: If your mirror has hanging loop like mine, be sure to position it next to the leaves. Press down to secure and let dry.

Rug Tufting with SIMJI

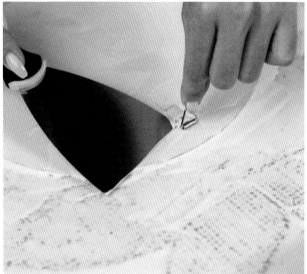

STEP 17: Cover the rug and the mirror with another generous layer of glue, taking care not to glue down the hanging loop. Apply the final backing fabric you cut earlier. Feel for the hanging loop, snip a slit with your scissors, and pull the loop through the fabric so that it's resting on top. Smooth the fabric, press down to secure, and then peel up the edges slightly. Let dry.

STEP 18: Carefully remove the rug and tufting cloth from the frame. Flip over the rug so that the tufted part is on top. Carefully cut off any excess tufting cloth.

STEP 19: Cover the mirror with the white circle you cut out earlier to protect it. Wearing a mask, shave the top of your rug to make it uniform. Snip any hanging yarn from around the edges.

Rug Tufting with SIMJI

STEP 20: Vacuum your rug. Clean the mirror, if desired. Roll a lint roller over the rug to make the colors pop! Hang it up on the wall where you'll pass by every day for a little pick-me-up.

TRY IT YOURSELF
GEODE MIRROR RUG

Now that you know how to tuft a mirror rug, the sky's the limit to what you can create with the same technique. I've included the designs for a cute Geode Mirror Rug in three color ways: pink, blue, and orange. You can choose whatever matches your décor. This is a great way to test the skills you just learned with a new design and a slightly harder shape for the mirror. I've included a condensed step-by-step here so you don't miss a step! You'll need all the same tools and materials as the Orange You Glad Mirror Rug, but different yarn.

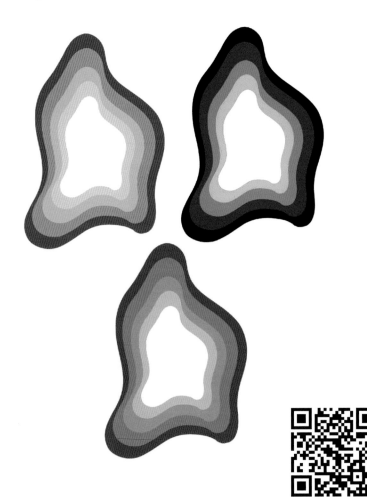

YARN COLORS

Neon pink

Deep pink

Bubblegum pink

Soft pink

Navy blue

Dark blue

Pacific blue

Turquoise blue

Caramel

Pumpkin

Mustard

Peach

STEP 1: Stretch your tufting cloth onto the tufting frame and download the Geode Mirror Rug template. Remember to flip the image horizontally! With the reflective side facing the tufting cloth, hold the mirror in front of the white center of the template to check sizing. Adjust the size of the projected image so that the mirror is 1½"–2" (3.8–5.1 cm) larger than the white space. This may be a little trickier than the orange mirror because the inner space is not a circle, but you got this! Use a marker to trace the image. Check your work before you move the projector.

STEP 2: Start with your darkest color yarn. Put it onto the yarn holder dowel on the frame or on the floor. Thread a strand of yarn onto the yarn-feeder loop near the top of your frame and pull the strand toward you. Make sure that your tufting gun is turned off and thread the yarn into the tufting gun. Then, outline the darkest, outermost section of the geode.

STEP 3: Next, color in the darkest section. Starting at the left side, tuft vertical lines from bottom to top until that section is completely filled in. Replace the darkest color with the second darkest and repeat the outlining process on the next section of the geode. Then, fill it in with vertical lines. Switch out the colors two more times and follow the same steps until the entire geode has been tufted. Take a moment to admire your work on the opposite side!

STEP 4: Vacuum the area behind the frame. Remove the clamps and place the frame on a table with the fluffy side down. Lay your mesh on top of the rug. Cut out a piece of mesh that is about 4" (10.2 cm) larger than the edges of your rug. Cut a similar-size piece of your final backing fabric for later. Set both aside. Pour a generous amount of glue onto your rug. Use your spatula to evenly spread the glue. Extend the glue about 2" (5.1 cm) past the edges. Use as much glue as you need to cover the rug thoroughly. Lay the mesh on top of the rug. Pour glue on top of the mesh, near the edges of the rug. Gently spread the glue from the edge of the rug outward, securing the mesh to the canvas. Let dry.

STEP 5: Use your scissors or a utility knife to remove the white center of your rug, taking care not to cut the tufted areas. Put it aside. Then, use your scissors to snip the edges of the tufting cloth to make them smooth. Line the center edge with glue, and gently spread outward 3"–4" (7.6–10.2 cm). Center the mirror reflective side down over the hole, with the hanging loop facing toward the narrowest side, and press onto the glue. Let dry.

STEP 6: Cover the rug and the mirror with another generous layer of glue, taking care not to glue down the hanging loop. Apply the final backing fabric you cut earlier. Feel for the hanging loop, snip a slit with your scissors, and pull the loop through the fabric so that it's resting on top. Smooth the fabric, press down to secure, and then peel up the edges slightly. Let dry.

STEP 7: Carefully remove the rug and tufting cloth from the frame. Flip over the rug so that the tufted part is on top. Carefully cut off any excess tufting cloth. Cover the mirror with the white center piece you cut out earlier to protect it. Wearing a mask, shave the top of your rug to make it uniform. Snip any hanging yarn from around the edges. Carve along the line where each color meets for a more finished look. It's time to clean up by vacuuming, cleaning the mirror, and rolling a lint roller over the rug. Then you're ready hang it up!

THRIFT LIFT
RUG PATCHES

I donate lots of clothing, but some items I just can't bear to part with—even if they live in the back of my closet. Can you relate? This project extends the life of those precious pieces and adds a little extra flair to your wardrobe. Win, win!

Size: Various sizes.
Mine were from 3"–7" (7.6–17.8 cm)

TOOLS & MATERIALS

Tufting cloth

Tufting frame

Thrift Lift Rug Patches template

Cell phone, tablet, or laptop

Projector

Adapter cable that can connect the projector to your device

Marker

Yarn (colors: red, pink, tan, black, and green)

Yarn threader

Tufting gun

Vacuum

Glue

Spatula

Scissors

Mesh

Utility knife (optional)

Carpet shaver

Tweezers

Clay tool (optional)

Lint roller

Painter's tape (or any other tape with minimal stickiness)

Wax paper

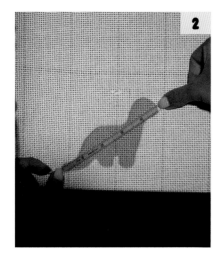

2

3

STEP 1: Stretch your tufting cloth onto the tufting frame, and download the Thrift Lift Rug Patches template onto your cell phone, tablet, or laptop, and then open the image. You'll see all four patches—one red heart, one pink heart, a dino nugget, and an alien—as one image. Flip the image horizontally. When you tuft, you will be working on the back side of the rug. Use an adapter cable to connect the projector to your device. Turn on the projector and point it toward your tufting frame so that the template appears on the cloth. Turn off the lights so that you can see the image clearly.

STEP 2: Examine the clothes that you want to enhance. For this project, I'm transforming a pair of denim overalls and two hoodies, but you can use any clothes that you want. Figure out where you want your rug patches to go, and then determine how big or small you want the patches to be. Adjust your image, smaller or larger, as you see fit.

STEP 3: Now, use the marker to trace your images. Trace any fine details first—like the eyes on the alien—and then trace the outlines for each patch. Check that you've traced the entire template. If so, turn on the lights. It's time to start tufting!

Rug Tufting with SIMJI

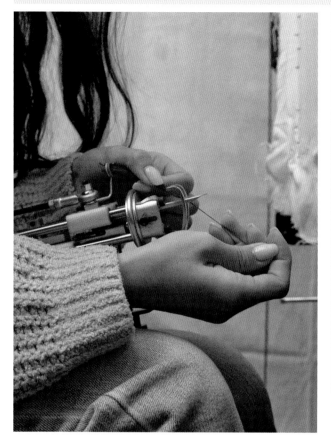

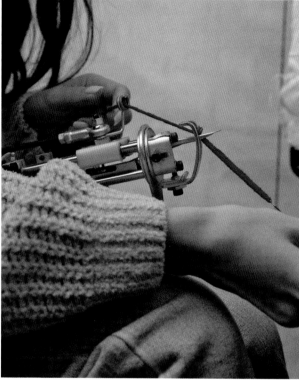

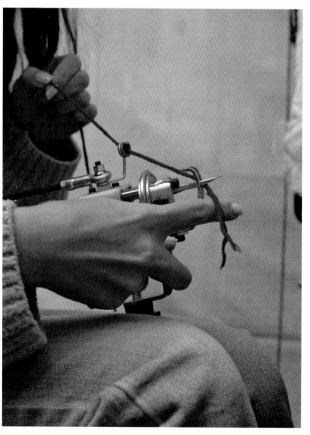

STEP 4: Let's begin with the hearts. Set up your red yarn by slipping it onto the yarn holder dowel on the frame. If you don't have a yarn holder, you can set the yarn on the floor. Thread a strand of yarn onto the yarn-feeder loop near the top of your frame and pull the strand toward you. Make sure that your tufting gun is turned off. Then thread the red yarn into the tufting gun.

TIP

Tufting Tip

If there's nothing in your closet you want to upcycle, try buying a few inexpensive pieces from a thrift shop.

Rug Tufting with SIMJI

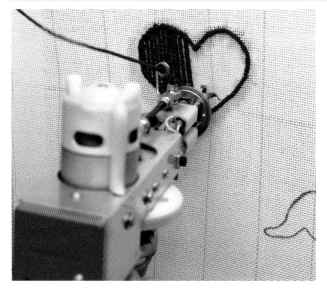

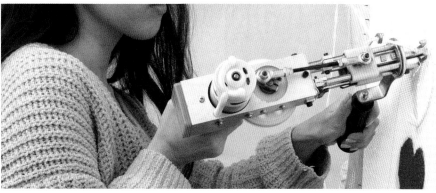

6

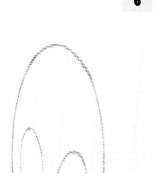

STEP 5: Turn on your tufting gun and adjust it to the slowest setting. Hold the handle for support and pierce the bottom center of one of the hearts, just inside the line. Press the trigger and tuft up the left side, following the line, until you reach the top center. Then, go back to the bottom center and tuft up the right side to complete the heart. Next, beginning on the left side, tuft vertical lines from bottom to top until the heart is completely filled in.

STEP 6: Replace the yarn on the dowel with pink yarn. Rethread your tufting gun with the new yarn. Outline and then fill in the pink heart as you did the red one. Take a peek at the two completed hearts on the other side of your canvas. Cute, right?

Back

Front

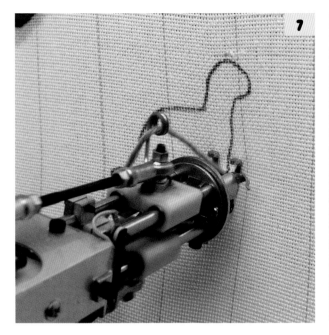

STEP 7: Replace the yarn on the dowel with tan yarn. Rethread your tufting gun with the new yarn. Let's outline the cute little dino nugget. Make sure your tufting gun is set to the slowest setting. Pierce the needle at the bottom center of the dino, just inside the line. Press the trigger and tuft counterclockwise, stopping at the top of the dino's head. Then go back to the bottom center and tuft up the left side to complete the dino.

STEP 8: Now, fill in the dino. Since the shape of the dino is mostly horizontal, it may be easier to tuft it horizontally. To do this, rotate your tufting gun 90 degrees to the right. Starting at the bottom left side, pierce the tufting cloth. With medium pressure, tuft in a straight line from left to right.

TIP

Tufting Tip

You can also tuft from right to left if it's more comfortable. And if tufting horizontally feels altogether weird to you, it's okay to tuft the dino vertically. Feel free to adjust your tufting angles as needed to fill in any small crevices.

STEP 9: Next up is our alien. Replace the yarn on the dowel with black yarn. Rethread your tufting gun with the new yarn. Outline the alien's mouth and eyes first, then fill in each eye. Beginning on the left side, tuft vertical lines from bottom to top until complete.

STEP 10: Replace the yarn on the dowel with green yarn. Rethread your tufting gun with the new yarn. Start at the bottom center and tuft up the left side until you reach the top center of the alien's head. Then go back to the bottom center and tuft up the right side to complete the shape. Outline the eyes and the mouth. Then, beginning on the left side, tuft vertical lines from bottom to top to fill in the alien.

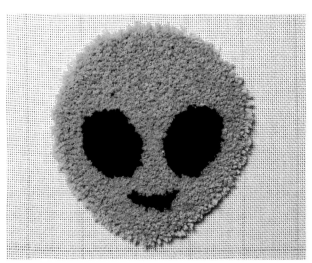

STEP 11: Vacuum the area behind the frame. Remove the clamps and place the frame on a table with the fluffy side down. Lay the mesh on top of your frame, and cut out mesh pieces for the mini rugs, making sure that the mesh is about 2" (5.1 cm) larger than the edges. Set everything aside.

STEP 12: Pour a generous amount of glue onto each rug. Use your spatula to evenly spread the glue. Extend the glue 1"–2" (2.5–5.1 cm) past the edges. Use as much glue as you need to cover the rug thoroughly.

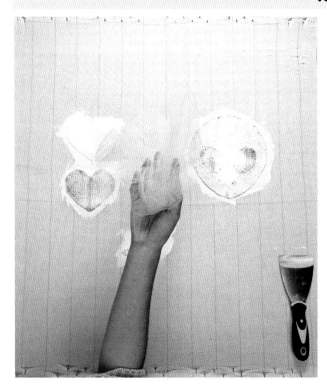

STEP 13: Lay the pieces of mesh on top of their corresponding rug patches. Pour glue on top of each piece of mesh, near the edges of the rugs. Gently spread the glue from the edge of the rugs outward, securing the mesh to the canvas. This keeps the mesh from moving around when you glue it down. Now, pour glue over the entire rug and spread it around. Flatten any wrinkles with your spatula as you secure the mesh to the rug and the canvas. Let dry for 24 hours or until dry.

Rug Tufting with SIMJI

STEP 14: Carefully remove the rugs and tufting cloth from the frame. Flip over the rugs so that the tufted part is on top. Take a minute to admire the cuteness! Now, you'll be using scissors to carefully cut out each rug. Fold the tufting cloth in between each patch to help you see where you should be cutting. Hold back the tufted yarn and cut the cloth as close and as evenly as possible to the rugs without cutting into them. Since we're not using final backing fabric on these rugs, flip them over to easily see the edge of the rug and where you should trim.

 TIP

Tufting Tip

I'm obsessed with the little dino nugget! Try not to trim it too perfectly to achieve the look and texture of a real chicken nugget. But do take care to trim enough fluff off the legs so that they are clearly defined.

15

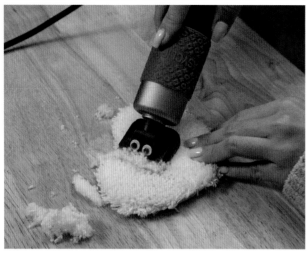

STEP 15: Wearing a mask, shave the top of each patch to make it uniform. Snip the hanging yarn from around the edges of the rugs. Then, angle your scissors and cut around the edges again, this time creating a slightly rounded bevel that is neat and sculpted.

Rug Tufting with SIMJI

STEP 16: Once we're finished shaving and trimming the edges of all of the rugs, let's do a little extra carving on the alien. First, use tweezers to separate any black and green yarn fibers that have become intertwined. You can also use a clay tool to push the fibers into place, as shown in the pictures, but it's not essential. Next, use a shaver to carve a clean line around the eyes and the mouth. Vacuum away any yarn dust as it gets in the way. When you are finished shaving, use your scissors to clean up the line, if necessary.

TIP

Tufting Tip

Carving is always optional. I personally love the look of a carved rug because it stays neat when touched, where the colors of a noncarved rug often intertwine. But again, it's all about personal preference.

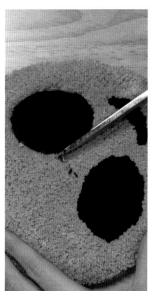

17

STEP 17: Vacuum each rug patch. Roll a lint roller over them to make the colors pop. Then, prep the clothing to be patched by rolling the lint roller over them, too.

STEP 18: Now, it's time to attach our patches. You can be super accurate (or not!), and you can place the patches wherever you'd like. Get creative. I chose the front pockets of a pair of denim overalls for my two hearts. The cute little dino nugget went on the top left of a cream-colored hoodie. And I placed my alien on the back of a black hoodie. Once you are satisfied with the placement of your patches, stick pieces of painter's tape around each patch to remember where they will go. Then remove the patches and put them to the side.

18

STEP 19: Tear off a sheet of wax paper for each patch. Place the wax paper underneath the fabric where you plan to attach your patch. You'll be gluing these patches, and the wax paper will protect against any glue seepage and accidentally gluing your clothes closed.

STEP 20: Put a generous amount of glue on the backs of your patches. Place each patch onto the designated areas you marked with tape (or just eyeball their placement), and then press firmly. Let dry for about 24 hours.

STEP 21: Remove the tape and the wax paper. Now, admire your work and show the cuteness off to the world!

 TIP

Tufting Tip

I used the same latex glue I use to back rugs since it can be used as fabric glue, and it's waterproof. Machine washing the glue is not recommended, though.

Rug Tufting with SIMJI

심지

TRY IT YOURSELF

SMILEY HAPPY PATCHES

It's about to get even cuter in your closet! Use your knowledge from the Thrift Lift Rug Patches to create four more adorable patches on your own. See the condensed step-by-step instructions, and feel free to add your own flair to these designs.

YARN COLORS

Yellow

White

Red

Dark green

Black

Pink

Sea green

STEP 1: Stretch your tufting cloth onto the tufting frame and download the Smiley Happy Patches template. Project the image onto the fabric. Remember to flip the image horizontally! Adjust the size of the projected image so that the patches will fit the clothes you wish to enhance. Use a marker to trace the images. Check your work before you move the projector.

STEP 2: Begin with any patch you'd like. Start with the yarn color for the smallest detail first. Put it on the yarn holder dowel on the frame or on the floor. Thread a strand of yarn onto the yarn-feeder loop near the top of your frame and pull the strand toward you. Make sure that your tufting gun is turned off and thread the yarn into the tufting gun. Tuft the small details first. For larger details, outline first, and then tuft vertical lines from bottom to top until the section is completely filled in. Rethread your tufting gun with different colored yarn as necessary. Do this for each patch.

STEP 3: Vacuum the area behind the frame. Remove the clamps and place the frame on a table with the fluffy side down to prepare for gluing. Lay the mesh on top of your frame and cut mesh for the mini rugs, making sure that the mesh is about 2" (5.1 cm) larger than the edges. Set everything aside.

STEP 4: Pour a generous amount of glue onto each rug. Use your spatula to evenly spread the glue. Extend the glue 1"–2" (2.5–5.1 cm) past the edges. Use as much glue as you need to cover the rug thoroughly, then lay the mesh on top of the patches. Pour glue on top of the mesh down the outer edges, then add more to the middle. Gently spread the glue from the edge of the rugs outward, securing the mesh to the canvas. Let dry for 24 hours.

STEP 5: Carefully remove the rugs and tufting cloth from the frame. Flip over the rugs so that the tufted part is on top. Carefully cut out each mini rug and then cut off any excess tufting cloth. Wearing a mask, shave the top of each rug to make it uniform. Snip the hanging yarn from around the edges of the rugs. Then angle your scissors and cut around the edges again, this time creating a slightly rounded bevel that is neat and sculpted. If desired, use a shaver to carve and fine-tune the details.

STEP 6: Vacuum each patch, then roll a lint roller over it to make the colors pop. Roll the lint roller over the clothes, too, to prep them to be patched.

STEP 7: Choose the placement for each patch and mark the areas with painter's tape. Place wax paper underneath the fabric where you want to attach your patches. Put a generous amount of glue on the backs of your patches. Place each patch onto the designated areas you marked with tape, then press firmly. Let dry for about 24 hours.

STEP 8: Remove the tape and wax paper, and you're done!

FOREVER FLOWER RUG

If you want something to last forever, you've got to put work into it. That's what I kept telling myself as I developed this project. I've never done anything like this but now I can proudly say that I have a flower that will last forever. And that I can vacuum. Soon you will, too. Let's go!

Size: Approximately 19" (48.3 cm) including the pot

TOOLS & MATERIALS

Tufting cloth

Tufting frame

Forever Flower Rug template

Cell phone, tablet, or laptop

Projector

Adapter cable that can connect the projector to your device

Marker

Yarn (colors: black, yellow, white, green, dark brown, reddish brown)

Yarn threader

Tufting gun

Vacuum

Mesh

Scissors

Final backing fabric (color: tan)

Glue

Spatula

1 18" (45.7 cm) bare stem wire

Wire cutters

Utility knife (optional)

Carpet shaver

Tweezers

Lint roller

Flower pot (any size)

Polystyrene foam half sphere (should fit snugly inside your flower pot)

Electric drill (or something to punch a hole in the foam)

3 18" (45.7 cm) paper-covered stem wires

Felt (color: dark brown)

Hot glue gun with glue stick (optional)

STEP 1: Stretch your tufting cloth onto the tufting frame, and download the Forever Flower Rug template onto your device and open the image. Flip the image horizontally. When you tuft, you will be working on the back side of the rug. Use an adapter cable to connect the projector to your device. Turn on the projector and point it toward your tufting frame so that the template appears on the cloth. Turn off the lights so that you can see the image clearly. I gave this template a blue background so that you can see and trace the white petals with ease.

STEP 2: Adjust the projected image to the size you prefer. The flower could be as big or as small as you want it to be. I chose a smallish to medium pot and I eyeballed the size of the flower to be about the size of the pot. Again, this is all personal preference, so do what makes you happy!

STEP 3: Use the marker to trace the image. Start with the details. In this case, trace the cute smiley face first, then move on to the middle circle and the petals. Next, trace the two leaves. Once you are finished, turn off the projector and check that you've traced the entire template. If so, turn on the lights and let's get to tufting.

STEP 4: We'll start with the smiley face. Make sure that your tufting gun is turned off. Thread the black yarn into the tufting gun.

TIP

Tufting Tip

Keep in mind that if you choose to make a gigantic flower, the rug will be heavier and you will need stronger stem wire, a bigger piece of polystyrene foam, and a larger pot to keep it standing.

Back

Front

STEP 5: Turn on your tufting gun and adjust it to the slowest setting. You'll be tufting in a tiny area, so you don't want to go too fast. Start with the cute little boba eyes. Hold the handle of your tufting gun for support and pierce the needle into the center of the small circle. Pulse the trigger, then twist the machine slightly counterclockwise (or clockwise, if it's more comfortable) and hold back to create more density. Do the other eye, and then tuft along the mouth of the smiley face.

STEP 6: Move on to the circle. Replace the yarn on the dowel with yellow yarn. Rethread your tufting gun with the new yarn. Pierce the tufting gun needle into the bottom center of the circle, just inside the line. Tuft around the circle. Outline the smiley face details next. Creating an outline will ensure that the eyes and mouth look polished. It will also make it easier to fill in the remainder of the circle. Since it is such a small area, you may not be able to tuft in rows. That's okay! Fill it in the best that you can, and trust the process.

TIP

Tufting Tip

A good rule of thumb is to tuft from smallest to largest details. When you are working on very fine details, such as our smiley face, hold your tufting gun firmly and resist tufting too quickly. Holding back a bit will result in slightly denser tufts and allow your small details to come through.

Projects 105

STEP 7: Now, let's outline the petals. Replace the yarn on the dowel with white yarn. Rethread your tufting gun with the new yarn. Pierce the tufting gun needle into the bottom center of the flower, just inside the line, and then tuft around the edges of the petals. Once you're finished, use the same yarn to outline the yellow circle.

STEP 8: Next, we'll color in the rest of the flower. Choose a petal. Begin at the outside of the petal and work your way in, tufting vertical lines from bottom to top until it is completely filled in. Repeat the process for all the petals. Once you've done that, check your progress on the other side.

Back

Front

Rug Tufting with SIMJI

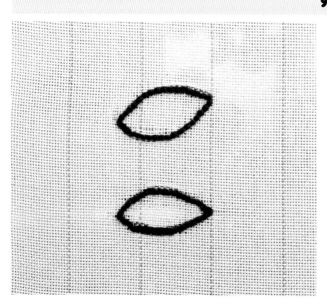

TIP

Tufting Tip

At some point on your tufting journey, you're going to tuft unevenly or you might notice a gap or two between rows. Don't stress over it. You can fill in gaps if you want to, but I suggest looking at the fluffy side of your project before making the decision. Fluff is very forgiving, and nine times out of ten, it's going to look amazing as is.

STEP 9: And, last but not least, we'll make our little leaves. Replace the yarn on the dowel with green yarn. Rethread your tufting gun with the new yarn. Just like we did with the flower, tuft around the outline of each leaf. Then fill them in, tufting vertical lines from bottom to top. If it's easier, you can try doing horizontal lines.

STEP 10: Vacuum the area behind the frame. Remove the clamps and place the frame on a table with the fluffy side down, to prepare for gluing. Lay your mesh on top of your rug. Cut out a piece of mesh that is about 2" (5.1 cm) larger than the edges of the rug. I used one piece of mesh for both the flower and the leaves. Now cut pieces of the tan backing fabric for the flower and leaves. Set all aside.

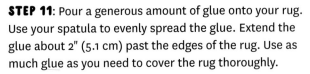

STEP 11: Pour a generous amount of glue onto your rug. Use your spatula to evenly spread the glue. Extend the glue about 2" (5.1 cm) past the edges of the rug. Use as much glue as you need to cover the rug thoroughly.

STEP 12: Lay the mesh on top of the rug. Pour glue on top of the mesh, near the edges of the rug. Gently spread the glue from the edge of the rug outward, securing the mesh to the canvas. This keeps the mesh from moving around when you glue it down. Now pour glue over the entire rug and spread it around. Flatten any wrinkles with your spatula as you secure the mesh to the rug and the canvas. Let dry for 24 hours.

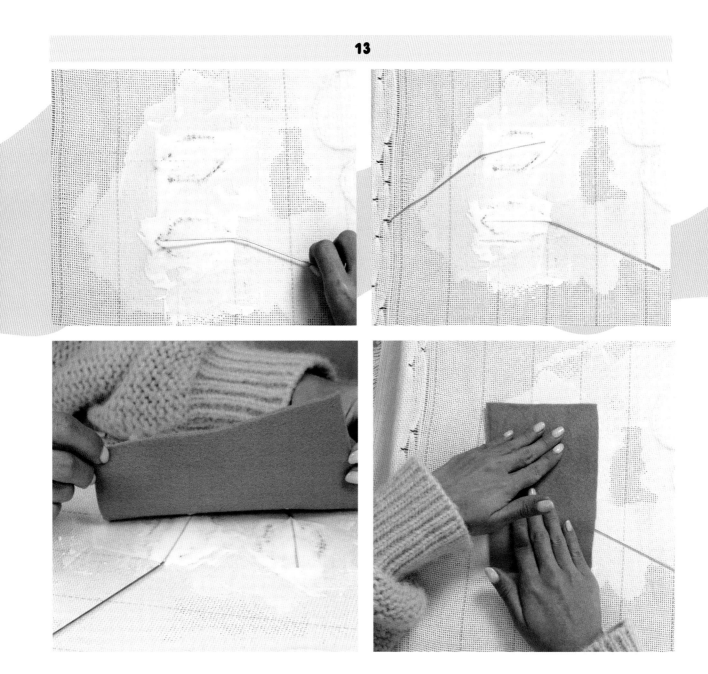

STEP 13: Let's make the stems for our leaves. Take the bare stem wire and clip it in half with the wire cutters. Put a slight bend in the wires, about the length of each leaf, and set aside. Cover the leaves with a generous layer of glue, making sure to extend the glue past the edges. Place your wires on top of the leaves, so that the bent part rests at the bottom center of each leaf. Now cover each leaf and bent section of wire with an extra-thick layer of glue. Place the tan backing fabric, which was cut to size earlier, on top of the leaves and wires. Press firmly, so that the wires and the edges of the leaves are securely adhered to the backing fabric. Set aside to dry for 24 hours.

STEP 14: Now cover your flower with a generous layer of glue, making sure to extend the glue past the edges. Place your other piece of final backing fabric on the flower. Smooth and press down, making sure that the edges are securely adhered. Let dry for 24 hours.

TIP

Tufting Tip

When securing backing fabric, really press into the crevices of the rug and run your fingers several times along the edges to ensure that you have a good seal.

  Rug Tufting with SIMJI

STEP 15: Carefully remove the rug and tufting cloth from the frame if desired. Since the pieces are small, you can cut them out without removing the cloth from the frame. Either way, flip over the rugs so that the tufted part is on top. Carefully cut off the excess fabric around each rug. Hold back the tufted yarn and snip the cloth as close and as evenly as possible to the rugs without cutting into them. Take extra care around the stem wires.

TIP

Tufting Tip

As you are cutting, flip your rug over every once in a while to check to see if your cuts are clean and your rug is shaped to your liking.

STEP 16: Shave the top of the flower to make it uniform. Now let's create a clean line between the white part of the flower and the yellow center. Carve around the yellow center with your shaver, while angling it toward the white part of the flower. Go around a second time, angling the shaver toward the yellow center. Vacuum away any yarn dust as it gets in the way. When you are finished shaving, use your scissors to fine-tune the line of the circle, if necessary.

Rug Tufting with SIMJI

STEP 17: Next, we'll work on the smiley face. First, use tweezers to separate any black and yellow yarn fibers that have become intertwined. This process makes it a lot easier to fine-tune the details. Take your scissors and snip around the mouth to carve a clean line. Now snip the hanging yarn from around the edges of the rug. Angle your scissors and cut around the edges again, this time creating a slightly rounded bevel that is neat and sculpted.

STEP 18: Shave the top of the leaves as you did the flower, taking care not to tug on the stem wires. Snip the hanging yarn from around the edges of one leaf. Then angle your scissors and cut around the edges again, this time creating a slightly rounded bevel that is neat and sculpted. Do the same for the other leaf. You can stop here, or you can carve veins into the leaves with your shaver as I did. Vacuum the flower and the leaves. Roll a lint roller over them to make the colors pop.

STEP 19: It's time to get the pot and stem ready. Place your half sphere of foam, flat side up, into the flower pot. Drill a hole through the half sphere. The diameter of the hole should be large enough to fit three paper-covered stem wires. Gather the paper-covered stem wires together, and push them into the hole as far as you can. Use your marker to mark the stem wires where they come out of the polystyrene foam. Figure out where you want to place the flower and leaves on the stem. I chose to put my leaves together, but you can arrange them however you like. It's art after all, right? And it looks so cute; we're almost there!

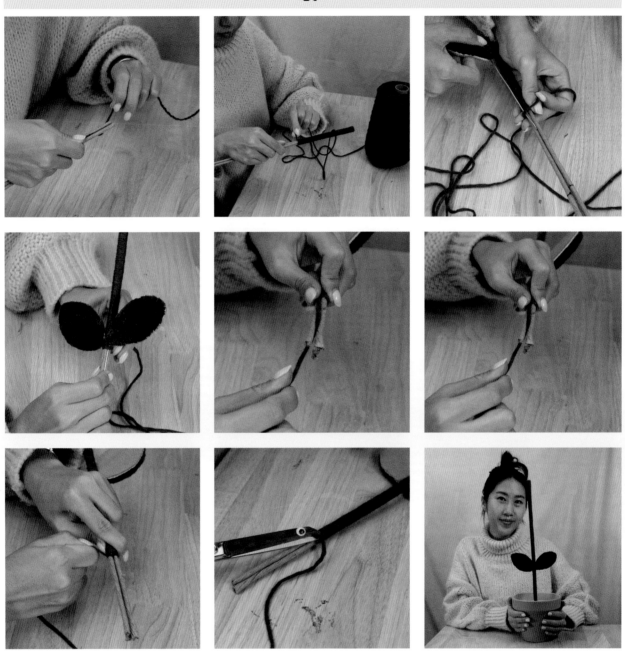

STEP 20: Gather your three paper-covered stem wires together, making sure that the place you marked is at the bottom. Tuck one end of the green yarn in between the stem wires at the top, and hold it in place with your thumb. Wrap the yarn tightly around the stem wires. Pause when you reach the point where you want your leaves to go. Slip each leaf wire in between the stem wires. Continue wrapping the yarn tightly around the stem wires until you reach the mark you made earlier. Tuck the end of the yarn in between the stem wires and pull it tight. Do that two more times, then snip the yarn close to the stem. It's really looking like a stem now.

TIP

Tufting Tip

I decided to use three stem wires to ensure that the stem is sturdy enough, but you can use more or fewer depending on the size of your flower.

Rug Tufting with SIMJI

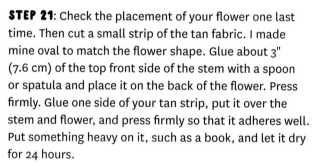

STEP 21: Check the placement of your flower one last time. Then cut a small strip of the tan fabric. I made mine oval to match the flower shape. Glue about 3" (7.6 cm) of the top front side of the stem with a spoon or spatula and place it on the back of the flower. Press firmly. Glue one side of your tan strip, put it over the stem and flower, and press firmly so that it adheres well. Put something heavy on it, such as a book, and let it dry for 24 hours.

TIP

Tufting Tip

Gluing only part of the flower to the stem gives you display options. For example, you might want to bend the top of the stem to make the flower face up or sideways and look as if it was floating–like a real flower. You couldn't do that if the entire flower was glued to the stem.

STEP 22: Trace the shape of the half-sphere onto the dark brown felt with marker, including the hole in the center. Cut out the shape. Pinch the center where the hole should be, and then snip a tiny X into the fabric. Hot glue the felt circle onto the flat part of the half-sphere, making sure that the X is over the hole. You can also use latex glue; however, hot glue will reduce drying time. Insert the half-sphere into your pot with the felt side up. Push the stem of your flower into the hole of the sphere. Add some latex glue to the stem if you want to make it extra secure. Add some fun texture by snipping different-size pieces of black, dark brown, and reddish-brown yarn into the pot.

Rug Tufting with SIMJI

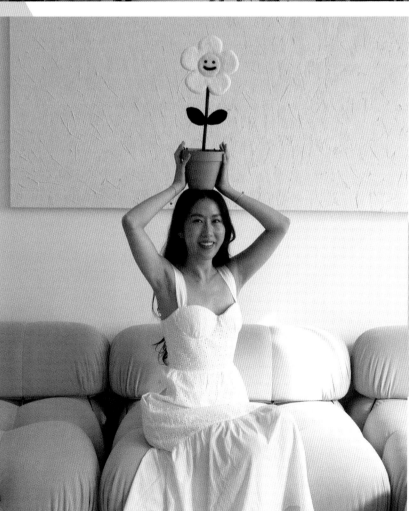

SPRING TULIP RUG

Now that you know how to create a Forever Flower Rug, why not add more to make a garden? Here are two more flower rugs for you to try on your own. This template allows you to experiment with different-size flowers. You'll need the tools and materials from the Forever Flower Rug, plus yarn in other colors for the new flowers.

YARN COLORS

Red

Gold

Green

Orange

Dark green

STEP 1: Stretch your tufting cloth onto the tufting frame and download the Spring Tulip Rug template. Remember to flip the image horizontally! Adjust the projected image to the desired size. Use a marker to trace the images. Check your work before you move the projector.

STEP 2: Begin with either flower. Start with the yarn for the smallest detail first. Put it on the yarn holder dowel on the frame or on the floor. Thread a strand of yarn onto the yarn-feeder loop near the top of your frame and pull the strand toward you. Make sure that your tufting gun is turned off and thread the yarn into the tufting gun. Tuft the small details first. For larger details, outline first, and then tuft vertical lines from bottom to top until the section is completely filled in. Rethread your tufting gun with different colored yarn as necessary. Do this for both flowers and leaves.

STEP 3: Vacuum the area behind the frame. Remove the clamps and place the frame on a table with the fluffy side down, to prepare for gluing. Lay the mesh on top of your frame, and cut mesh for the mini rugs, making sure that the mesh is about 2" (5.1 cm) larger than the edges. Cut a similar-size piece of the tanbacking fabric. Set both aside.

STEP 4:

Pour a generous amount of glue onto each rug. Use your spatula to evenly spread the glue. Extend the glue 1"–2" (2.5–5.1 cm) past the edges. Use as much glue as you need to cover the rug thoroughly. Then lay the mesh on top of the patches. Pour glue on top of the mesh, first taking it down on to the outer edges, then pouring more onto the middle of the rugs. Gently spread the glue from the edge outward, securing the mesh to the canvas. Let dry for 24 hours.

STEP 5:

For each flower, clip a bare stem wire in half and bend each half slightly. Cover the leaves with a generous layer of glue, place a stem wire on each leaf, then cover it with more glue. Place the tan backing fabric on top of the leaves and bent part of the wires. Press firmly, so that the wires and the edges of the leaves are securely adhered to the backing fabric. Set aside to dry for 24 hours.

STEP 6:

Cover the flowers with a generous layer of glue, making sure to extend the glue past the edges. Place your other piece of final backing fabric on the flower. Smooth and press down, making sure that the edges are securely adhered. Let dry for 24 hours.

STEP 7:

Carefully cut out the flower pieces without removing the cloth from the frame. Flip over the rugs so that the tufted part is on top and then cut off any excess tufting cloth. Shave the top of each rug to make it uniform. Snip the hanging yarn from around the edges of the rugs. Angle your scissors and cut around the edges again, this time creating a slightly rounded bevel that is neat and sculpted. If desired, use a shaver to carve and fine-tune the details.

STEP 8:

Vacuum each piece then roll a lint roller over it to make the colors pop.

STEP 9:

Prepare the pot and the stems for each flower. Drill a hole through the half sphere large enough to fit the paper-covered stem wires. Gather the paper-covered stem wires together and push them into the hole as far as you can. Use your permanent marker to mark the stem wires where they come out of the foam. Repeat this step for the second flower.

STEP 10:

Assemble the paper-covered stem wires and leaf for each flower. Wrap with yarn as discussed in the main project tucking the yarn in tight before you begin. Do that two more times, then snip the yarn close to the stem. Repeat this step for the second flower.

STEP 11:

Attach each flower to its stem. Cut a small strip of the tan fabric. Add glue to the top front side of the stem and place it on the back of the flower. If your flowers are on the larger side, 3" (7.6 cm) is enough. A smaller flower may need less glue. Press firmly. Glue one side of your tan strip, put it over the stem and flower, and press firmly so that it adheres well. Put something heavy on it, such as a book, and let it dry for 24 hours. Repeat this step for the second flower.

STEP 12:

Trace the shape of the half-sphere onto the dark brown felt with permanent marker. Snip a tiny X into the fabric where the hole should be. Glue the felt circle onto the flat part of the half-sphere, making sure that the X is over the hole. Insert the half-sphere into your pot with the felt side up. Push the stem of your flower into the hole of the sphere adding glue for an extra-strong hold. Add some fun texture by snipping different-size pieces of black, dark brown, and reddish-brown yarn into the pot. Repeat this step for the second flower. Place your potted garden wherever you need a little sunshine!

TWO-TONED MINI TOTE

For this project, I decided to create a classic bag with a neutral vibe for the minimalist in me (and you). Deep down, I know she's in there somewhere! Honestly, this bag would also look great in bright color combos like pink and orange. So, if you can't find your inner minimalist, go for the max.

Size: Approximately 13" (33 cm) including handle

TOOLS & MATERIALS

Tufting cloth

Tufting frame

Two-Toned Mini Tote template

Cell phone, tablet, or laptop

Projector

Adapter cable that can connect the projector to your device

Marker

Yarn (colors: green, beige)

Yarn threader

Tufting gun

Latex glue

Spatula

Scissors

Utility knife (optional)

Carpet shaver

Mesh

Final backing fabric (color: tan)

Tweezers

Vacuum

Lint roller

Iron

2 gold O-rings

Hot glue gun and glue sticks

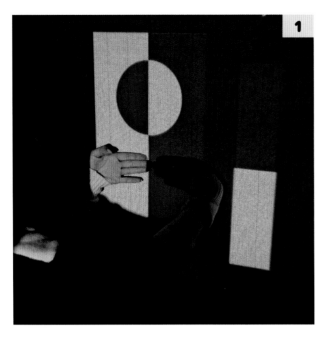

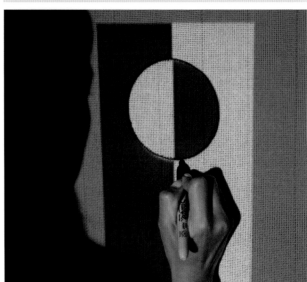

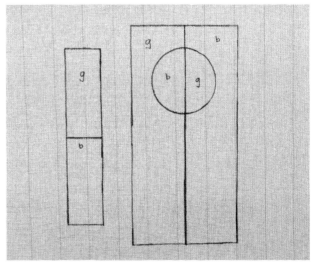

STEP 1: Stretch your tufting cloth onto the tufting frame, and download the Two-Toned Mini Tote template onto your device, and then open the image. You'll see the two parts of the bag as one image—a large rectangle, which is for the tote part, and a small rectangle, which is for the strap. Flip the image horizontally. When you tuft, you will be working on the back side of the rug. Use an adapter cable to connect the projector to your device. Turn on the projector and point it toward your tufting frame so that the template appears on the cloth. Turn off the lights so that you can see the image clearly. We'll be folding this tote bag in half the long way. Determine how big or small you want the tote pouch to be. Adjust your image, smaller or larger, as you see fit.

STEP 2: Now use the marker to trace your images. Trace the circle on the large rectangle first and then trace the outlines for each piece. To avoid making a mistake, I marked the areas of the rug that will be green with a G and the beige areas with a B. Once you are finished, check that you've traced the entire template. If so, turn on the lights. It's time to start tufting!

TIP

Tufting Tip

Since your rug will be two-toned, rather than simply tracing down the vertical line running through the middle of the template, trace just to the right of one color and then switch. This will give you a clear guide for tufting both colors. Do the same thing with the horizontal line in the center of the strap.

Rug Tufting with SIMJI

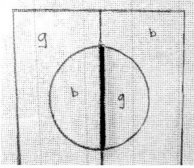

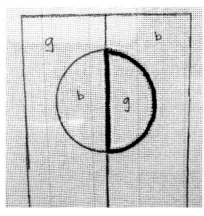

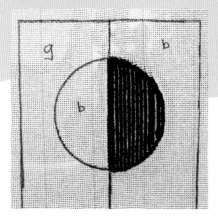

STEP 3: Let's begin with the green half of the circle. Set up your green yarn by slipping it onto the yarn holder dowel on the frame. If you don't have a yarn holder, you can set the yarn on the floor. Thread a strand of yarn onto the yarn-feeder loop near the top of your frame and pull the strand toward you. Make sure that your tufting gun is turned off. Then thread the green yarn into the tufting gun.

STEP 4: Turn on your tufting gun and adjust it to the slowest setting. Hold the handle for support and pierce the bottom center of the green part of the circle, just inside the line. Press the trigger and tuft up the center line until you reach the top. Then go back to the bottom center and tuft up the right side of the circle to complete the outline. Then, tuft vertical lines from bottom to top until the half circle is completely filled in. For this project, try to keep the lines somewhat close together. We want this rug to feel dense and luxurious.

TIP

Tufting Tip

If you can't decide between color combinations, tuft a couple of small patches off to the side of your frame so you can visualize them. It's actually a huge timesaver. Imagine getting halfway through your project and then deciding that you don't like the colors! It would take forever to pull out all that yarn and start over.

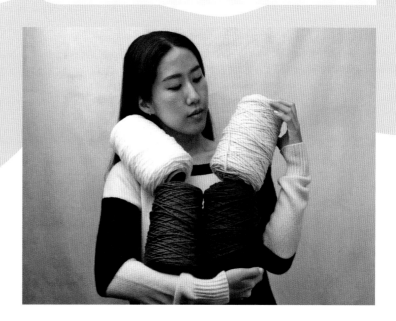

5

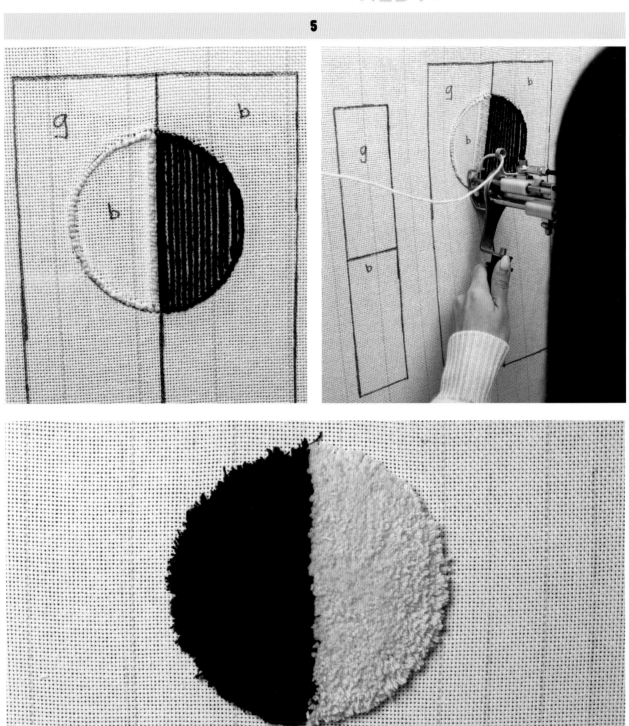

STEP 5: Replace the green yarn on the dowel with beige yarn. Make sure your tufting gun is off and rethread your tufting gun with the new yarn. Outline and then fill in the beige half of the circle as you did the green side. Take a peek at the completed circle on the other side of your canvas. I love it!

Rug Tufting with SIMJI

6

7

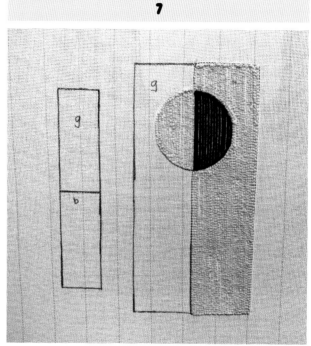

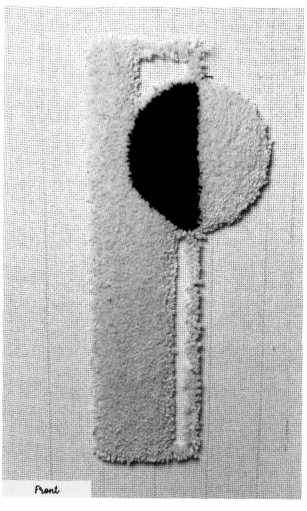

Front

STEP 6: Next, let's outline the green half of the circle with the beige yarn. Pierce the needle into the bottom center of the circle. Press the trigger and tuft around the green half, pausing at the top of the circle. Outline the rest of the beige side of the rectangle.

STEP 7: Now fill in the beige. Starting at the bottom right side of the rectangle, pierce the canvas with your tufting gun. With medium pressure, tuft vertical lines from bottom to top until the area is filled in, stopping every once in a while to check your work.

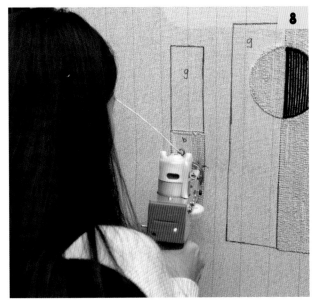

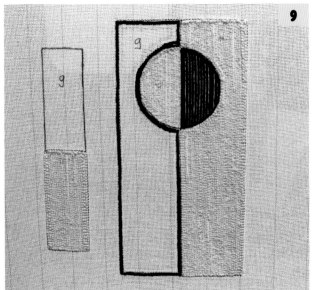

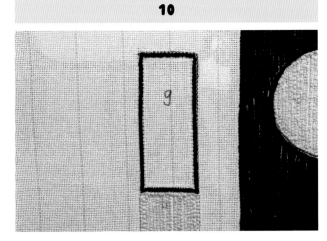

STEP 8: Let's keep it going with the beige. Outline the beige part of the strap. Then tuft vertical lines to fill it in.

STEP 9: Replace the beige yarn on the dowel with green yarn. Rethread your tufting gun with the new yarn. Starting at the bottom center of the large rectangle, outline the green half of the rectangle, making sure to carefully go around the beige circle. Then fill in the entire green half of the rectangle the same way you did on the beige side.

STEP 10: Outline the green part of the strap. Tuft vertical lines to fill it in. Now take a peek behind your canvas. It's really starting to take shape, right?

TIP

Tufting Tip

Some manufactured tufting frames can stretch fabric unevenly due to wide gaps between nails. Don't worry if your tufted lines aren't pin-straight. Your rug will still look neat and clean on the fluffy side.

Front

Rug Tufting with SIMJI

STEP 11: Vacuum the area behind the frame. Remove the clamps and place the frame on a table with the fluffy side down to prepare for gluing. Lay the mesh on top of your frame, and cut mesh for the tote and strap, making sure that the mesh is about 2" (5.1 cm) larger than the edges. Next, cut the final backing fabric so that it is about 2" (5.1 cm) larger than the edges of the tote part of the rug only. You won't need it for the strap. Set everything aside.

STEP 12: Pour a generous amount of glue onto each part of the rug. Use your spatula to evenly spread the glue. Extend the glue 1"–2" (2.5–5.1 cm) past the edges. Use as much glue as you need to cover the rug thoroughly.

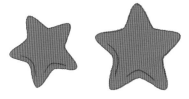

STEP 13: Lay the mesh on top of the tote and strap. Pour glue on top of the mesh, near the edges of both parts of the rug. Gently spread the glue from the edge of the rugs outward, securing the mesh to the canvas. This keeps the mesh from moving around when you glue it down. Now pour glue over both pieces of the rug and spread it around. Flatten any wrinkles with your spatula as you secure the mesh to the rug and the canvas. Let dry for 24 hours.

STEP 14: Thoroughly cover the tote section of the rug with another generous layer of glue. However, this time, coat the edges but don't go beyond them. Cover the tote with the final backing fabric you cut earlier. Smooth the fabric and press down to secure, and then slightly peel up the edges on the long sides so that they remain free. Let dry for 24 hours. There isn't backing fabric on the strap.

14

TIP

Tufting Tip

For this project, use slightly less glue than you normally would to attach the backing fabric so that the backing fabric remains hidden when the tote is constructed. You can always add more glue, little by little, if you need to. However, it's much harder to remove glue from a rug than it is to add it.

STEP 15: Carefully remove the rug and tufting cloth from the frame, or you can simply cut them out without removing the cloth from the frame. Next, separate the strap rug from the mini tote, being careful not to cut into the backing fabric on the tote. Flip over the rugs so that the tufted part is on top. Carefully cut off the excess fabric around the strap. Hold back the tufted yarn and snip the cloth as close and as evenly as possible to the rug without cutting into it. Set it aside.

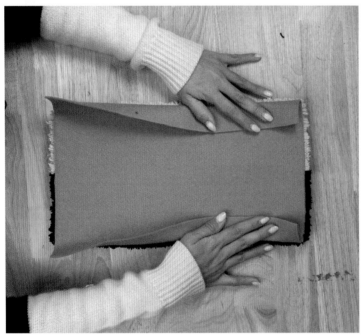

 TIP

Tufting Tip

When carving between two colors next to each other, always carve twice—first with the shaver angled toward one color, then again with the shaver angled toward the other color.

STEP 16: Now remove the excess tufting cloth from the large rectangle. Cut the tufting cloth as close and as evenly as possible to the rug, but keep the backing fabric intact on the long sides of the rectangle. Fold the extra backing fabric into the rug, and then fold the rug in half to get a hint of what your mini tote will look like when it's finished!

STEP 17: Shave the top of the tote and the strap to make the tufts uniform. Then run your scissors through the dense tufts, lightly snipping where the colors meet to make room for your shaver. Angle your shaver a bit toward one color and then the other to carve between the two colors to form a clean line. Vacuum away any yarn dust as it gets in the way. Repeat for the strap.

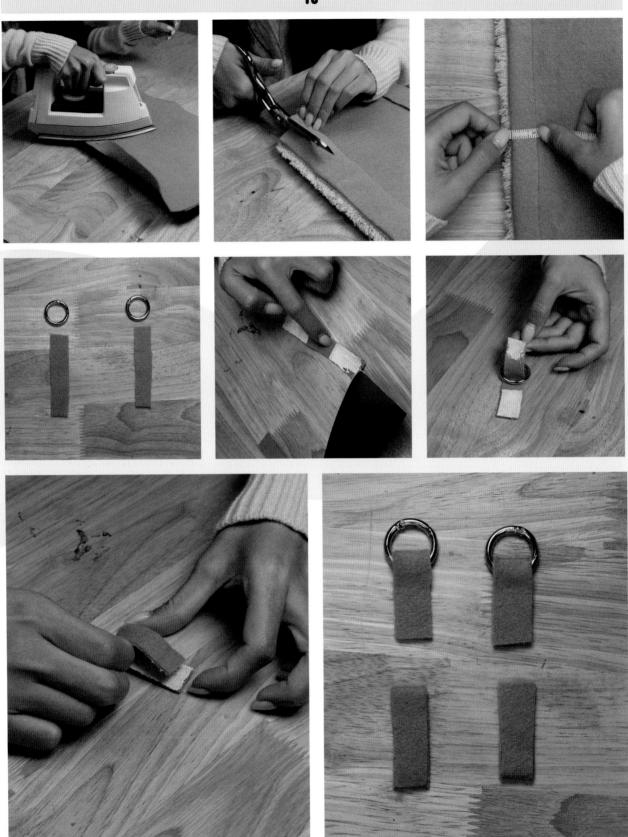

Rug Tufting with SIMJI

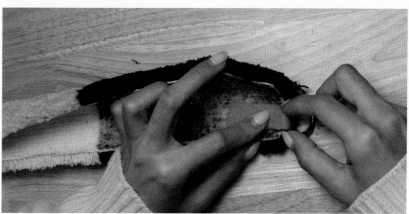

STEP 18: Let's get ready to make our tote bag! First, fold the backing fabric flaps in and iron them down flat. This will help the gluing process later. Then trim each flap so it is about ¾" (1.9 cm) wide. Try to trim in one continuous strip, as we will be using it to make loops that will attach your strap to the bag. Cut four strips 1.5" to 1.75" (3.8–4.4 cm) long when folded in half from the scraps. Grab your O-rings and slip them onto the strips. Glue each end of the strips and then press them closed so that the ring is locked in the loop. Do the same with the last two strips, only without the rings. Set the four looped tabs aside to dry for 24 hours.

STEP 19: Grab your large rectangle rug. Place it on the table in front of you with the circle at the top. Flip the rug over so that the back is facing you. Put a generous amount of glue on the two tabs with the rings. Place one tab at the top right of the rug, just next to the flap. Press firmly until it adheres to the backing fabric. Put the other tab on the top left side of the rug, next to the flap.

Press firmly until adhered. Set aside. Now let's glue the remaining tabs onto the strap. If you have extra O-rings, you can put them on the loops temporarily to help guide your placement, like I did. Hold the strap lengthwise and then fold it in half so that it kind of looks like a hot dog bun. Open it back up, and glue one tab on either end of the bun, just below the crease. When placing them, keep in mind that you want the ring to elegantly graze the edge of the rug when it's finished. Let everything dry for 24 hours.

 TIP

Tufting Tip

It pays to be patient! You can use hot glue to put together your tote bag and skip the drying time. However, latex glue is stronger and will last longer.

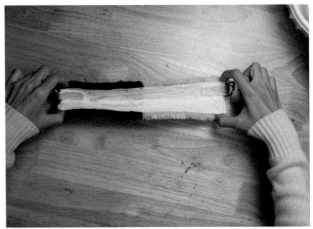

STEP 20: Once dry, tug on the tabs of your strap to make sure that they are secure. If so, then cover the back of the strap rug with a generous amount of glue. Add extra glue on and around the looped tabs. Fold the rug in half lengthwise, so that it looks like a hot dog bun. Place it on a table and press the rug firmly so that it adheres. Put something heavy on it, such as a cutting board with a weight or some books, so that it remains closed while drying. Set aside to dry for 24 hours.

STEP 21: Time to form the mini tote! Use a spatula to spread glue along the top of the previously ironed flaps. The goal is to glue flap to flap when you fold the mini tote rug in half. In general, you don't want to get glue on the yarn, but if you accidentally do, like I did, don't stress. The next part of the process will hide it. Now fold the rug in half crosswise, so that the flaps meet each other. You'll notice that the flaps may wrinkle in areas. When this happens, I use a knitting needle to hold them in place or smooth them out. If you don't have a knitting

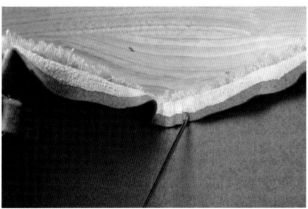 

needle, though, you can use any other slim tool. Press firmly, particularly near the bottom corners, and smooth out the wrinkles so that you have clean edges on the sides of your tote. Again, put something heavy on top of it so that it remains closed while drying. Set aside for 24 hours. Once it's dry, it will look like a bag!

TIP

Tufting Tip

Glue the flaps only one-half to three-quarters of the way to the edge. This will prevent glue seepage from accidentally gluing your bag closed.

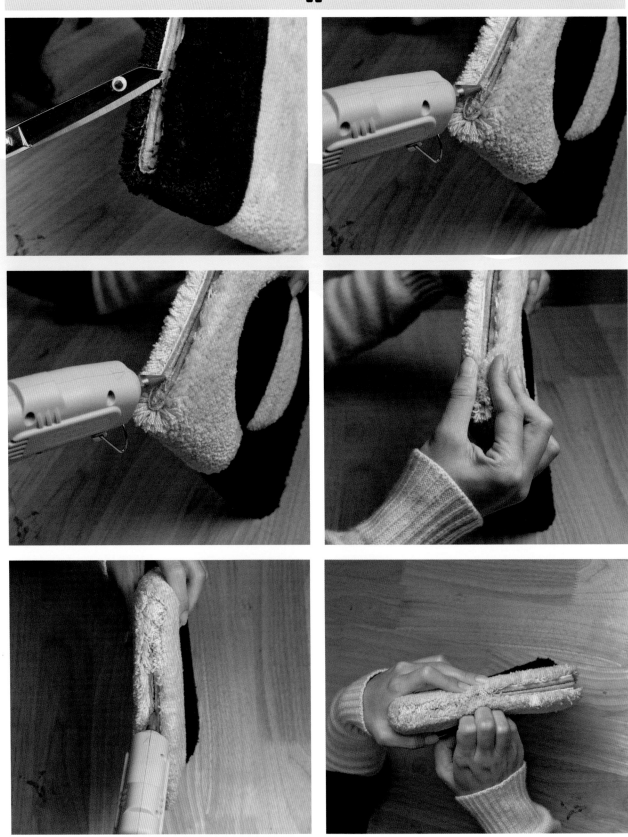

Rug Tufting with SIMJI

STEP 22: Now that your bag is dry and sturdy, we can work on the details. Trim off any little crunchy areas where you may have gotten glue. Now we are ready to hide the seams. Apply a small, thin line of hot glue on one seam, and then press the yarn together so that it covers the seam. Be careful not to burn your fingers! Keep going, step by step, until you reach the top of the bag. Add a little more glue wherever it's needed. Repeat the process on the other side of the bag. Check the bottom of the bag. If you can see any of the white tufting cloth, put a bit of hot glue on the white part, and then press the yarn together, as you did for the seams, to cover it. When you are finished, sculpt around the edges of the bag with your shaver to make them rounded and neat. Fine-tune with scissors, if necessary.

TIP

Tufting Tip

To avoid crunchifying the yarn on your bag, use as little hot glue as possible. To hide the seams, squeeze together your yarn from the base as much as possible so the ends can remain free and flowy.

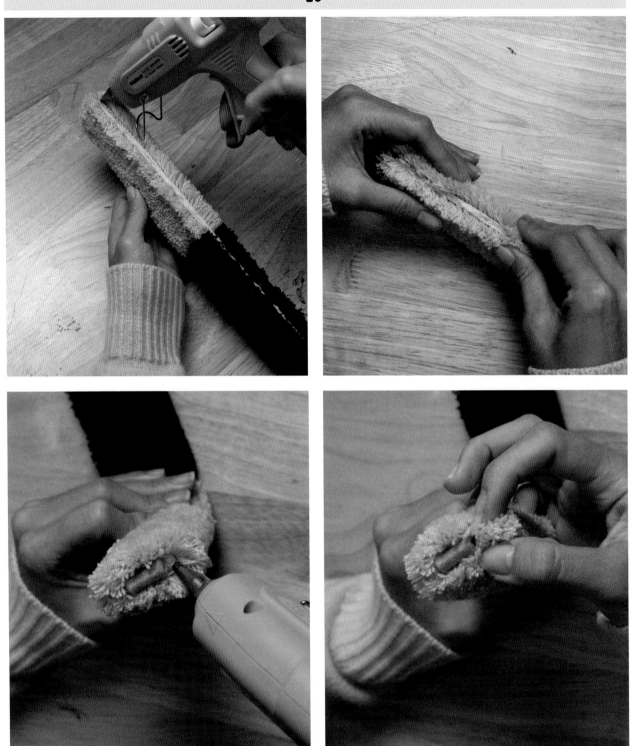

STEP 23: Repeat the same gluing-and-squeezing-yarn process to hide the seams on the strap. Pay special attention to the ends where the tabs are. Sculpt the edges with a shaver or your scissors. Then vacuum away the dust, attach the strap, and take yourtwo-toned mini tote out for a spin.

Rug Tufting with SIMJI

SUMMER VIBES PURSE

I made this bag for a SpongeBob themed event! I added a circular bamboo handle for the summery vibes but you can swap out the handle for wood if you like. You could also change the colors up for a different effect—light orange and hot pink would be so cute! Or you could create cloud vibes with cream and light blue. Follow the condensed step-by-step instructions. I know you can do it!

YARN COLORS

Muted Lime

Green

Cream

HANDLE

Bamboo or wooden circular handle

STEP 1: Stretch your tufting cloth onto the tufting frame and download the Summer Vibes Purse template. Adjust the size of the projected image to the desired size. Use a marker to trace the images. Turn on your lights to check your work before you move the projector.

STEP 2: Place the green yarn on the yarn holder dowel on the frame or on the floor. Thread a strand of yarn onto the yarn-feeder loop near the top of your frame and pull the strand toward you. Make sure that your tufting gun is turned off and thread the yarn into the tufting gun. Outline first, and then tuft vertical lines from bottom to top until the green areas are completely filled in.

STEP 3: Vacuum the area behind the frame. Remove the clamps and place the frame on a table with the fluffy side down to prepare for gluing. Lay the mesh on top of your frame and cut, making sure that the mesh is about 2" (5.1 cm) larger than the edges. Next, cut the final backing fabric so that it is about 2" (5.1 cm) larger than the edges of the rug. Set everything aside.

STEP 4: Pour a generous amount of glue onto the rug. Use your spatula to evenly spread the glue. Extend the glue 1"–2" (2.5–5.1 cm) past the edges. Use as much glue as you need to cover the rug thoroughly. Then lay the mesh on top. Pour glue on top of the mesh first taking it down onto the outer edges, then pouring more onto the middle of the rugs. Gently spread the glue from the edge of the rug outward, securing the mesh to the canvas. Let dry for 24 hours.

STEP 5: Coat the rug with another layer of glue. However, this time, coat the edges but don't go beyond them. Cover the rug with the final backing fabric you cut earlier. Smooth the fabric and press down to secure, and then slightly peel up the edges on the long sides so that they remain free. Let dry for 24 hours.

STEP 6: Cut out the rug without removing the cloth from the frame, being careful not to cut into the backing fabric. Flip over the rug so that the tufted part is on top. Remove the excess tufting cloth and the backing fabric off the top of the rug. Next, move your scissors along the sides of the rug, cutting only the excess tufting cloth and keeping the backing fabric intact.

STEP 7: Shave the top of the rug to make it uniform. Snip the hanging yarn from around the edges of the rug. Then angle your scissors and cut around the edges again, this time creating a slightly rounded bevel that is neat and sculpted. Vacuum away any yarn dust.

STEP 8: Fold the backing fabric flaps in and iron them down flat. Then trim each flap so it is about ¾" (1.9 cm) wide. Cut one strip from the backing fabric scraps. Slip the bamboo circle handle onto the strip then glue the stip closed so that the handle is locked in the loop. Set the looped handle aside to dry for 24 hours.

STEP 9: To form the purse, use a spatula to spread glue along the top of the previously ironed flaps. Now fold the rug in half crosswise, so that the flaps meet each other. Smooth out any wrinkles. Put something heavy on top of it so that it remains closed while drying. Set aside for 24 hours.

STEP 10: Apply a small, thin line of hot glue on one seam, and then press the yarn together so that it covers the seam. Be careful not to burn your fingers! Keep going, step by step, until you reach the top of the bag. Add a little more glue wherever it's needed. Repeat the process on the other side of the bag. Check the bottom of the bag. If you can see any of the white tufting cloth, put a bit of hot glue on the white part, and then press the yarn together, as you did for the seams, to cover it. When you are finished, sculpt around the edges of the bag with your shaver to make them rounded and neat. Fine-tune with scissors, if necessary.

STEP 11: Glue the tab with the circular handle inside using latex glue or hot glue. Don't glue the entire tab to the inside of the purse, you want the handle to have a little bit of free range of motion.

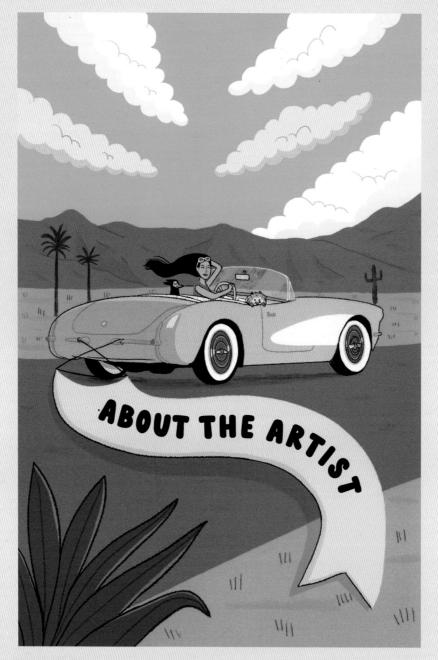

ABOUT THE ARTIST

SIMJI is a textile artist, content creator, and "rugfluencer." She shares her popular rug-tufting videos with millions of viewers around the world on TikTok, YouTube, and other social media outlets at @simjiofficial. Born in South Korea and raised in Los Angeles, SIMJI creates fun and intricate pop culture–inspired pieces, pet portraits, food-related rugs, and much more.

Recognizing the need for relatable and entertaining rug-making content, SIMJI pioneered a new approach toward reaching and educating aspiring rugtufters. By combining her passion for rug making with an entertainment-based perspective, SIMJI successfully bridges the gap between artistry and adience, captivating viewers with her unique content and expanding herinfluence within the industry and beyond.